FAR FROM
OVER

FAR FROM OVER

THE UNOFFICIAL STORY
by DALTON HIGGINS

THE MUSIC
AND LIFE OF
DRAKE

ECW PRESS

Published by ECW Press
2120 Queen Street East, Suite 200, Toronto, Ontario, Canada M4E 1E2
416-694-3348 / info@ecwpress.com

LIBRARY AND ARCHIVES CANADA CATALOGUING IN PUBLICATION

Higgins, Dalton
Far from over : the music and life of Drake, the unofficial
story / Dalton Higgins.

ISBN 978-1-77041-001-5
ALSO ISSUED AS: 978-1-77090-253-4 (PDF); 978-1-77090-254-1 (ePUB)

1. Drake, 1986-. 2. Rap musicians—Canada—Biography.
3. Actors—Canada—Biography. I. Title.

ML420.D762H63 2012   782.421649092   C2012-902725-1

Cover design: Rachel Ironstone
Cover image: Kristian Dowling/PictureGroup
Text design: Tania Craan
Printing: Friesens   5   4   3   2   1

The publication of *Far From Over* has been generously supported by the Canada
Council for the Arts which last year invested $20.1 million in writing and publishing
throughout Canada, and by the Ontario Arts Council, an agency of the Government
of Ontario. We also acknowledge the financial support of the Government of Canada
through the Canada Book Fund for our publishing activities, and the contribution of
the Government of Ontario through the Ontario Book Publishing Tax Credit. The
marketing of this book was made possible with the support of the Ontario Media
Development Corporation. the Canada Book Fund.

PRINTED AND BOUND IN CANADA

To my right hand Karen Bell-Higgins, and my two little (growing) feet, Shiloh and Solomon Bell-Higgins. And my tiny inner village, mom and dad, Pearlita and Josiah Higgins, and my brother, Milton The Mayor.

TABLE OF CONTENTS

Introduction

His moment had arrived. It was August 1, 2010, on a warm, overcast summer day in Toronto. I was standing elbow-to-elbow with other reporters, mostly aging hip hoppers and hipsters, part of a deafening audience at the Molson Amphitheatre for a rap concert. But it wasn't just another concert. It was the first large-scale rap gathering hosted by Aubrey Graham, known to the world as Drake, for a new festival he helped birth called OVO (October's Very Own). And to those in the know it was his official hometown coming-out party.

If the Grammy nominations and platinum-certified debut album hadn't yet made his influence clear, the enthusiastic crowd of young people chanting his hard-edged yet sensual lyrics word for word certainly spoke volumes. That the concert at the amphitheater — a venue with more than five times the capacity of his previous show just over a year earlier — appeared sold out, spoke even louder. Torontonians may be better known for their love of home-grown rock 'n' roll and hockey, but today it was proud to celebrate an unlikely hometown hero.

While he looked like a big American rap star, dressed casually in his own OVO-branded varsity jacket, he sounded familiar with his unusual hybrid rap delivery mixing the cadence of the American South with a Toronto intonation. He was speaking directly to a new breed of North American youth — a group that is digitally engaged, a lot more hopeful. The audience was a surprising mix — a United Nations of teens to 30-somethings who saw something of themselves in the biracial black Jewish kid, raised just a few miles northeast of the amphitheater.

Women vastly outnumbered the men in attendance. While onstage, Drake effortlessly played to his devoted female constituency, once proceeding to kiss an unnamed young lady onstage, as the crowd went wild.

By the end of his 90-minute set of hits from his debut album, *Thank Me Later*, and his enormously successful mixtapes, just when raging Drake fans could have gone home happy, two of the biggest rap icons of the last 15 years — Jay-Z, who many expect to become the first rap billionaire, and Eminem, SoundScan's Artist of the Decade (32 million albums sold in the past 10 years) — came onstage to do cameos as his *special guests*. The hot summer day suddenly sizzled, the roar of the crowd took over, the ground seemed to shake. When Jay-Z and Eminem spat their verses from rap anthems "Forever" and "Run This Town," any Drake doubters couldn't help but be swayed. Hogtown had a first-class hip hop artist who was one of their own.

Raised in the tony Forest Hill neighborhood — where average houses go for just over $1 million — Drake didn't have the hard-scrabble childhood of most rap stars. In a CNN interview, Drake tried to explain his unlikely rise to the top: "Part of the whole appeal of me as an artist, I did have things that were seen initially as strikes against me, being from Canada, being an actor, being light-skinned, being Jewish, all of these things that I guess in the stereotypical rap world don't really fit the package."

But even as a teen, Drake had his eye on hip hop success: he once wrote in his school yearbook that his favorite expression was "bling, bling," and that his goal was to become a break-dancer and singer. Funny when school yearbook projections actually start to come to life. By the time he was 13, Aubrey Graham already knew something about success, having secured a starring role on Canadian cult TV favorite *Degrassi: The Next Generation*. It was only a matter of time before the driven, talented performer found similar success with his other passions. The hook on his 2011 single "Headlines" perfectly summed up his rapid ascent.

Drake set himself apart long before he had inked a record deal, releasing most of his early music on the internet and using social media as his primary marketing tool. For an aging music industry veteran born before the '90s like me, Drake made me truly understand, first hand, how the music industry of yesteryear was now officially done like the Nets' stay in New Jersey. Another biracial musical wunderkind, Prince, whom Drake's musician uncle Larry Graham Jr. mentored, prophesized the coming of a Drake, almost two decades earlier. The artist used his powers of pop prognostication to predict a day when musicians would have more creative control over their art and would connect directly with their fans. So when Drake nabbed two 2009 Grammy Award nominations for

Best Rap Song and Best Rap Solo Performance for his song "Best I Ever Had," before even releasing a full-length CD, it seemed Prince's prediction had come to pass. By the time soul iconoclast Stevie Wonder agreed to record harmonica parts on Drake's sophomore release, *Take Care*, and show up as a special guest at his hometown OVO festival, it was clear to fans, industry execs and artists alike that Aubrey Graham was someone who warranted close attention.

As an urban music journalist for the last 15 years, I've paid special attention to Drake, a kid who grew up in a neighborhood a hop, skip and jump from my own. In 2007, my colleague Urban Music Association of Canada President Will Strickland and I decided to book Drake to perform in an Urban X-Posure hip hop artist showcase for up-and-comers in downtown Toronto, and even as experts in our field, we didn't anticipate how popular he'd be.

Harbourfront Centre's Brigantine Room venue was completely jammed with Drakephiles (most of them female), and we wondered where exactly this Drake Nation had come from. What stood out for Strickland about Drake is what also continues to amaze me. He was one of the most humble young celebs I'd ever met, and I've met many, from obscure wannabes to *Billboard* chart-toppers. "I remember him sending me the longest, realest text message ever, apologizing for being only four minutes late to the [Urban X-Posure] event audition," remarked Strickland. "Only four minutes late. And this is the music business, where things don't exactly run on time. He showed up to the auditions and paid his $25 application fee, and stood in line like everybody else. He could have played the *Degrassi* superstar-guy role. But he wasn't interested in that. That showed me he respected the process of making it." If you were to apply the textbook definition of success to Drake's entertainment career to date, despite him being only in his mid-20s, it's safe to say he is well on his way to making it — whatever *making it* means — or that to many he has already made it. Made it cool to dream large and ignore the banal. He just wants to be successful. Growing up, I never expected to live to see a black president. Or a Toronto rapper make it this big in America.

Drake has a tattoo that carries an acronym with the inscription YOLO (You Only Live Once), a new lexicon that he promotes in his song "The Motto" and that is enjoying wide public use — its inscription showed up on Jordan Brand sneakers worn by Brit broadcaster Tim Westwood, and even *High School Musical* actor Zac Efron has it inked on his right hand. It was an idiom Drake picked up from one of his partners-in-rhyme, Rick Ross, who he's collaborated with on his own solo recordings, and it speaks clearly to his life mission of not being afraid to dream, not being afraid to put himself out there, to go for broke, which is why this biography is just the beginning of Drake's larger-than-life story.

GROWING UP DRAKE:

Graham Family Values

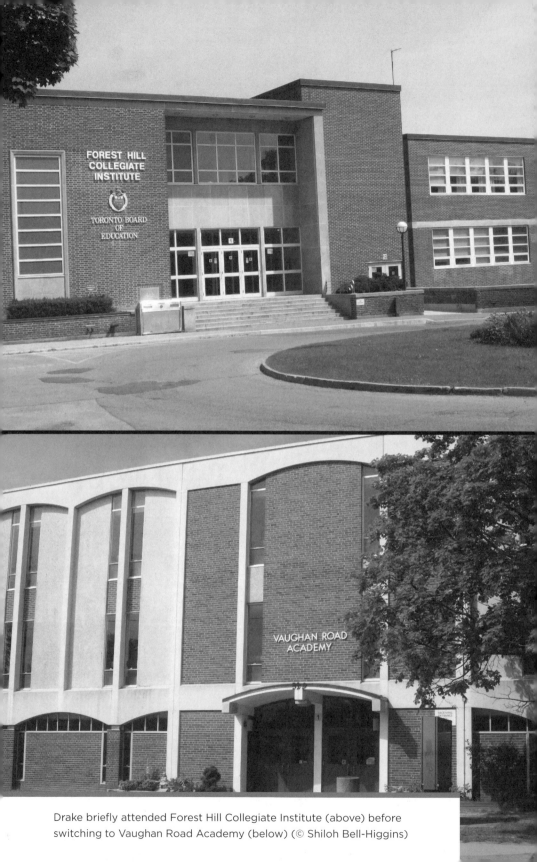

Drake briefly attended Forest Hill Collegiate Institute (above) before switching to Vaughan Road Academy (below) (© Shiloh Bell-Higgins)

Aubrey Drake Graham was born on October 24, 1986, the only child to an African-American musician father, Dennis Graham, who lives in Memphis, Tennessee, and a spirited white Jewish educator mother, Sandi Graham, who raised him in Toronto's predominantly Jewish Forest Hill neighborhood. She said that though he "was very fussy," he was a unique toddler who seemed very comfortable in the spotlight and loved to entertain. "We always thought there was something very different about this kid," Sandi admitted to *Degrassi Unscripted.* "When we had a piano at home and I would come home with my nursery rhymes, Aubrey at three years old would take the lyrics and he would change them. . . . I realized then that other kids just didn't do that."

The Graham household proudly displays photos of Drake's earliest playful forays into music. Included in this collection were pictures of Drake as a young child holding his first microphone and guitar (of the prescient picture, Sandi noted, "He was probably practicing for me"). There were also pictures from his dad's side of the family lying around, including one great picture of Drake sitting on his dad's lap, and another of his iconic musician uncle Larry Graham Jr.

Drake's parents split up when he was only five years old, and because he was raised as an only child by his single mother, Sandi tried to keep him busy to mimic familial support. "Being an only child I always had him in a lot of activities," she said. "Whether it was day camp, group activities, hockey, a lot of things where he'd have to learn to be a team player." Looking back as a young adult, Drake reflected on his mother's successful strategy to keep him feeling engaged, focused and productive as an only child: "My mom signed me up for dance classes, piano lessons. She was trying to do anything to keep me occupied. Her main objective was keeping me from being aimless, just wandering the streets. She signed me up for hockey, basketball, music, dancing. I tried piano, I tried guitar and I couldn't stick with anything — until acting became my main focus."

Encouraged by his good looks as a child and preternatural preschool charm, Sandi got a young Aubrey involved in TV and theater early on. "When Aubrey was about five years old I took him to this agent, and she really liked Aubrey, so he did print work, and a catalog, and a couple of commercials." Sandi also enrolled him in programs at Toronto's Young People's Theatre. While Drake downplays the influence of these early experiences on his present-day acting skills, observing, "It was really just a bunch of young kids acting really hyper, and then we'd throw on masks and call it a play," there's reason to believe it played a role in laying out a blueprint for success in the acting world.

Drake does remember a shift between costumed playtime and his first really successful play, the theater's production of *Les Misérables*. He believed the audience enjoyed the production beyond the novelty of seeing a bunch of kids performing their hearts out. "*Les Mis* was the first thing that people actually liked, and came to see, and clapped for a good reason, not like, 'Yay, it's over, good let's go home,'" he said.

Early theatrical aspirations aside, Drake genuinely enjoyed music as a child too, and growing up with strong musical bloodlines certainly didn't hurt. Drake had some heavily decorated music and entertainment influences in his life, especially on his African-American side. His dad, Dennis, who called the great boxer Muhammad Ali a friend, was a drummer for Jerry Lee Lewis. "My dad is very musically gifted, a lot of soul," Drake told MTV. While his father is not as visible on the music scene these days, he can be seen in a guest cameo in a rap video by Drake's cousin Chris "Royalty" Graham. These musical connections meant that Drake was around high-level musicians from the time he was a child. His father takes some credit for his musical awareness at a very young age. "I used to hold him in my lap and I used to hold him in my office while I played the piano," he told Memphis's *Action News* 5. "This is how it got started." Dennis also thinks there's a correlation between his son's lyrical abilities and hanging around in Memphis, a city that's birthed such great songwriters as Isaac Hayes.

This artistic integrity and musical pedigree went even further: Drake is also the nephew of two musical greats who had a hand in helping to shape the soul and R&B canon that Drake's generation now sample in their hip hop. One uncle, Larry Graham Jr., was the bassist in Sly and the Family Stone and played with Prince. And in the '70s another uncle, guitarist Mabon "Teenie" Hodges, added his silky rhythm-and-blues-based guitar lines to help develop what is known as the Memphis Sound. Hodges, who might be better known to his nephew's generation as having played on Cat Power's brilliant *The Greatest*, is actually responsible for co-writing more than a few timeless, monster soul hits like "Love and Happiness" and "Take Me to the River" with the incomparable Al Green. Drake has also said in interviews that his grandmother babysat Louis Armstrong. Given that his family tree was filled with rock 'n' soul royalty, there's no question that some musical skill would trickle down.

Though he spent summers with his dad's side of the family in Memphis, family rituals might include bonding on Appleville, at Shelby Drive and Neely. He hung out with his dad while the elder Graham was gigging, exposing Drake to new music and making him privy to the inner workings of Memphis's Royal Studios, where seminal soul producers and vocalists like Willie Mitchell and Al Green created musical magic. Certainly his exposure to what was going on in Memphis musically helped trigger some of his early inspiration to start performing.

His dad had instilled in him the rigors of living the musician's lifestyle as a child. "My dad was always a musician," he told a NARAS (National Academy of Recording Arts and Sciences) gathering in Nashville about some of his earliest experiences and memories as an entertainer. "My first time performing I was really young, probably like eight or nine, and he had taken me out when he wasn't supposed to (because he had a gig and he was looking after me), and he thought it would be interesting to bring me up onstage to sing the one song that I knew, which was 'Ride, Sally, Ride.' So I ended up onstage performing with my dad, and everyone in the place thought it was the cutest thing in the world. I don't remember much about my childhood, but I remember that night."

As an adult, Drake is aware how that regional music influenced his sound. "I was there at a very great time, a very influential time," he told *Urb* of his years spent taking in the Memphis rap sounds that informed his early art, and of being exposed to low-income neighborhoods like Orange Mile and the Peppertree Apartments. "Around the ages of like 12, 13, 14, 15 . . . I was there sort of just soaking it all in. It was around the time when Memphis actually had a dope movement, before Kia Shine had that 'Krispy' song, they were actually hailing Yo Gotti, Kink and Skinny Pimp . . . you know, 8 Ball and G, Three 6 Mafia was doing their thing. It was great." Dennis noted the soul music songwriting influence on his son, suggesting that Drake's "metaphors are so phenomenal now, because he's been in Memphis."

While his father's side played a key role in his early musical development, Drake had inherited some musical chops from the maternal side of his family as well. He told *JVibe*, a bimonthly magazine for Jewish teens, that his cousins on his Jewish side were "very skilled in piano and graduated from arts and music schools." Drake also believed that his mom may have unconsciously influenced his songwriting process and vocal delivery. "My mom used to force me to say things as colorfully as possible," he said. "She would never let me get by with saying, 'Well, that food was good.' No, I had to say, 'That food was delicious,' or something extravagant. My mom was responsible for a lot of the way I write, the way I choose to say things. That's where the music comes in on my mom's side."

His mother said that by the time he was 10 years old, he began writing his own music material — and it was original. "He brought to my attention that what makes his work different is that he writes his own lyrics; that's an incredible gift."

Drake's grandma, or *bubbe*, also played a role in Drake's understanding of language and words — a key part of any rapper's songwriting arsenal. "We went to visit his grandmother in a nursing home," explained celebrity photographer Jonathan Mannion, of his experience snapping some pictures of Drake and his grandmother for MTV. "It was really a conversation between them and they were talking about how they used to do crossword

Drake and his mother, Sandi, at the 2011 Juno Awards
(© Robin Wong/PR Photos)

puzzles and learn-words together. . . . And she was like, 'It's really paying off now.'"

Even with the love and support of his mother and her family, Drake felt an imbalance because his father wasn't around as much as Drake would have liked. "I remember for a lot of my life, being ashamed of who I was, or not confident in who I was, sort of, just different things, like the fact that I was more emotional than other kids," admitted Drake on MTV's *Better Than Good Enough* documentary on his life. "I used to cry a lot in school. I used to fall for girls so hard. And be so reluctant to embrace those emotions." At times growing up Drake also had to deal with the tension of being biracial in a homogenous white Jewish school environment. In Forest Hill, sometimes the only black and Filipino people one might see routinely were women working as nannies carting around Jewish kids. Drake felt that kids didn't really accept him fully as a biracial kid with black roots. He told *Heeb* magazine that kids would call him a *schvartze*, which is an anti-black Yiddish slur.

Because Drake attended school with the sons and daughters of millionaires in Forest Hill, his mother says the perception of his wealthy childhood upbringing actually clashed with the reality. Drake's mom suffered from rheumatoid arthritis, a condition that prevented her from working as much as she would have liked. "People have this perception that he came from a privileged background. Certainly he had a lot of support, but when other kids had computers we were going to the library. The reality is he worked very, very hard. Nothing is magic," she told IndustryMag.com. "There was something very old school about Drake," she recalled, in that everything he got he earned through good old-fashioned hard work.

Maintaining a relationship with a geographically distant father, who wasn't readily available for significant male guidance, forced Drake to grow up fast. In an interview with ABC News, he spoke about the struggles of his childhood. "I was actually hurt by a lot of the things that happened throughout the course of my life," Drake told ABC's Darius Brown. "I had to become a man very quickly and be the backbone for a woman who I love with all my heart, my mother."

For Drake, family has always come first, and his preoccupation with keeping his loved ones close to him at all times all seems to begin and end with his mom. "Everything good in life I get from my mom, you know," Drake told MTV. "The desire to be intelligent, kind, caring . . . it's like a constant thing on my mind, because of my mom, you know, and the fact that she's such a great woman and I don't think she was ever loved properly." He added, "She's been the most supportive person I've ever had in my life — the only person that loves me unconditionally, really. I know a lot of people love me and I love a lot of people. But to love somebody unconditionally is different."

Drake recorded a song on his sophomore *Take Care* release titled "Look What You've Done" as a heartfelt lyrical homage to his mom and *bubbe*'s contribution to his life. He punctuates the hook of the catchy piano-laden song by repeating "I got you," which hip hop listeners know means, "I will protect you and take care of you from here on in."

Things with his father were more complicated. "I saw my dad get arrested by a SWAT team at the border for trying to cross over," he told ABC News about a visit gone awry when his father couldn't enter Canada due to his criminal charges in the United States. He added, "I've seen things that didn't make me happy. They were character building. That's why I think people in the 'hood can still connect with what I'm saying even though I'm not saying, 'Yeah I got crack in my pocket,' 'cause that wasn't my struggle necessarily, [but] I speak from a place that's just human emotion."

Noted for his ability to write profound, heartfelt, accessible rhymes at a time when drug-addled, expletive-filled bluster is now considered potent song writing, Drake has spent many years perfecting his songwriting craft based on his own life experiences.

"I've been writing since I was really young," he told *Scene and Heard*. "I wrote about how I viewed the world, like not having my dad around or being biracial. I would never write about things I don't know about, like the 'hard' street of Toronto. It's always relative to my life and other people can relate." Drake's art has always closely mirrored his reality, and the personal details that make it into the songs are what give Drake's smooth lyrics their depth. For example, his dad's financial woes show up in songs like "Look What You've Done" and "The Calm," where he admits to having to send money to his father via Western Union. It's that honesty, that realism that made Master Gee, one-half of the legendary Sugarhill Gang, mark Drake as "one of the brightest lights in contemporary rap music right now." Gee explained, "As far as people telling stories, he tells stories. You can listen to his stuff and tell that there is some sort of telling of an experience, painting a picture. I appreciate a lot of the younger rappers, but unfortunately, I see the lyrical content going another way, if you will . . . you have a floor when you're a rapper, an emcee, and you want to take people on a journey like Drake."

Part of his family's narrative of struggle provided some of the grist for his early songwriting forays. Arguably, by him witnessing firsthand some of the harsher aspects of life from his dad, it opened up a part of his brain that might not have otherwise been tapped into. When his dad had hit rock bottom and landed in jail for "an assault charge or a drug charge or something," Drake began scribing some potent rhymes as an artistic outlet during visitations. "My dad was in jail for two years and he shared a cell with this dude who didn't really have anyone to speak to," he told *Complex* magazine. "So, he used to share his phone time with this dude and at the time I was probably 16 or 17, this dude was like 20 or 22, and he would always rap to me over the phone — it was Poverty, that was his rap name."

Poverty might have been an unusual mentor, but he inspired Drake to process his emotions and experiences in a new way. "I started to get into it and I started to write my own shit down," he said of the prison visitation after-effects. "[Poverty] would call me and we would just rap to each other. And after my dad got out I kept in touch with the dude and eventually . . . I accepted the fact that I wanted to be in music."

Back home in Toronto, far away from the struggles of his dad's life, Drake attended Forest Hill Junior and Senior Public School for his elementary schooling and Forest Hill Collegiate Institute, a public high school just northwest of downtown Toronto. He might be an A-list celebrity now, but in high school he was just another teen who felt like he didn't fit in. "It was very awkward," he commented to the *Toronto Star* about being considered a racial minority at school. "I never had a girlfriend. Not one of those girls would bring me home. It would be too risky."

Despite much of the perception in the public realm about Drake being a kind of modern-day Fresh Prince of Forest Hill who had everything easy, the reality of the situation was that by the time Drake was in his mid teens he felt awkward and not so attractive being a biracial kid in a mostly white school environment. "I used to have this terrible afro . . . it made me look like I had the biggest head in the world," he told MTV's *When I Was 17*. His longtime friend Niko had to intervene and hook Drake up with his first proper barber, J. Mac. After the haircut, Drake said he felt "reborn." Niko even confessed that he initially thought Drake was a "big loser," adding, "He'd borrow his uncle's car and lie and tell people that it was his."

His other major influences were the R&B and rap stars whose careers he was following with more interest than your average teen boy. Some of these figures could be found on a table he had that carried images of everyone from Barry White and the Notorious B.I.G., all the way to Nas and Pharrell Williams. Drake said Williams played a big role in him wanting to create a more unique brand of urban music. "I remember being 17 and I started to really fall in love with the whole Star Trak movement," he said on MTV's *When I Was 17* of the record label started by Williams and his fellow producer Chad Hugo. "Pharrell and his whole movement really made me care about music." Drake was also allegedly smitten with the rap flows of a few of Bad Boy Records' roster of rappers from Harlem, both Mase and Loon, who had perfected a sluggish yet meticulous drawl in their lyrical delivery. It could be argued that he incorporated elements of this Supa Dupa rap flow — that rapper Big Sean reportedly reinvented years later — by utilizing one-word punch lines and rhyme schemes. Spurred by his other rap idols like B.I.G., Drake filled Hilroy notepads with pages and pages of song ideas and lyrics, then practiced his creations on the in-house studio microphone in his mom's basement.

After a few years of demonstrating his rhyme and vocalizing skills in private, Drake decided to go out on a limb in 2003–2004 and help form an R&B/hip hop mash-up group called the Renaissance. Members included now Grammy-winning songstress Melanie Fiona, his friend and current keyboardist Dalton "Dio" Tennant and talented local vocalist Aion Clarke, a.k.a. Voyce Alexander. The group would sometimes rehearse at Fiona's manager Carmen Murray's condo located in the ritzy Bay and Bloor area of Toronto, and they had an artist residency at the popular Avocado Supper Club in downtown Toronto. Fiona described it as "this really nice underground place," while Drake summed it up as "this restaurant that was really popping in Toronto," noting the celebrities that used to come through, like ANTM champ Eva Marcille Pigford and actress Meagan Good. "I remember one night we were performing upstairs and they were shooting 'Pon De Replay,' Rihanna's first video," reminisced Drake.

Fellow band member Voyce, who was just as new to the whole professional "live" public performance thing as Drake, loved the experience. "At this point I had never even been downtown; I was still a young sheltered church boy," he recalled. "I was very green to everything. I was like, 'Yeah, money, I can make my own money and sing secular music, yeah sounds fun!' So we went down there, and they loved us, and we started doing little sets here and there."

The chemistry between the group was undeniable. Fiona told the U.K.'s *Hip Hop Chronicle* how excited she was to get the opportunity to work with a still-developing Drake and "just to make a couple bucks during the week . . . we loved creating and working together, and it was great." Voyce says Drake was the ultimate emcee and host to some of the gigs, especially as the youngest member of the group. "Drake would come back and be like, 'Welcome to Avocado, thank y'all for coming out this evening,' and he was funny and witty, and then I would sing, and he would rap, and Melanie would come and sing a nice song. And then me and Melanie, we would do a duet. It was a complete show, people would be coming out of the woodwork to come see us."

The Renaissance was booked to play between one to three days a week, playing mostly cover songs. The band reportedly never attempted to record or chase a record deal. They were more like a glamorized cover band, with individual members working on their own solo materials. Voyce explained, "The Renaissance music repertoire might be I was singing John Legend, Al Green. Melanie would come in and sing some Alicia Keys or Etta James's 'At Last.' And then Drake would come in and we'd do 'Tainted' by Slum Village, and he would spit a verse in between me singing that. It was a mixture of old school and new school, that's why we connected."

Even with this supper club success, things turned sour quickly, especially for Drake. "One night I was in my mom's living room, and I got a phone call from the manager," he told MTV's *When I Was 17*. "And she was like, 'I'm sorry, I hate to be the one to do this but I just got to tell you, you're out of the group. I don't think music is your calling.'" Having someone in a professional context boldly tell Drake that, despite years of writing songs, his music ability was just not up to par was bad enough, but getting kicked out of a group he helped start made it worse. "My heart dropped. I was shocked when I got kicked out. I was like the OG member." Despite being devastated by the news, at the time, he described this experience as a great "character builder." The group disbanded a few weeks after Drake got kicked out.

Years later, in February 2011 during the NBA All-Star weekend in Los Angeles, the Renaissance had an unplanned all-star reunion of their own. Fiona was charged with singing the Canadian national

The Renaissance group members Dalton "D10" Tennant, Drake, Melanie Fiona and Aion "Voyce" Clarke (© Aion Clarke)

anthem at the game, while Voyce sang the anthem at the slightly less visible Saturday-night festivities. Drake was in Los Angeles the same weekend and stopped by for the game. The former members chatted briefly and snapped a rare photo of them together.

The band breakup, while disappointing, was only a temporary setback that wouldn't stop Drake. In fact, it might've arguably made him hungrier for success. The lack of control that got him fired from the budding supergroup likely strengthened his conviction that a DIY approach was the way to go. Drake and his mother began handling the marketing, distribution and promotion of his music, mimicking the independence that many of the Memphis-based artists he admired exuded. "I personally pretty much do everything, along with my mom," Drake told *Notable Interviews*. "My mother helps me with the mixtapes, like sending them out to people, and that's real cool that she takes an interest like that."

Most ambitious young artists would have headed south of the border at this point, much like his former Renaissance bandmate Fiona, who left for Los Angeles and found success there, eventually earning Soul Train and Grammy awards. But that approach wasn't going to happen for the rising star just yet. "We can sit and talk about the Toronto mentality for days and days," he remarked on Flow 93.5 FM's now-defunct *OTA Live* show. "But at the end of the day, I appreciate this place more than any other place in the entire world."

Relocating to Memphis might have been easy, given his dad's roots there. Memphis had already birthed many legendary black musical greats and a King of Rock 'n' Roll. But it seems he had reason to believe that a new musical king could emerge from elsewhere, namely Toronto.

THE
DEGRASSI
YEARS

By the time he had reached eighth grade, Drake had been involved in the arts almost as long as he could remember, but it took just one job to transform him from an amateur actor to a certified star. His big break came from a rather ordinary place: his elementary school classroom. While attending Forest Hill, there was a kid in his class whose father happened to be an agent looking for new talent. "'If there's anyone in the class that makes you laugh, have them audition for me,'" said the dad, according to Drake. The charismatic teen took him up on the offer, and, "after the audition he became my agent." The agent arranged some auditions, including one for a role on a TV show in a hyper-successful franchise, *Degrassi: The Next Generation*. Now, auditioning for a Canadian TV series is one thing. It's another thing to be considered for a role on *Degrassi*. The Canadian drama that follows the lives of a group of teenagers who lived on or near Degrassi Street in Toronto wasn't just a TV show, it was a cultural institution. The series, shot in Toronto since its debut in 1979, gained a solid reputation for helping youth, not just in Canada, but around the world, interpret their own identities. One of the show's strengths lies in its ability to openly discuss complicated issues like teen pregnancy, domestic violence, eating disorders, drug use and homosexuality, making it miles ahead of primetime TV fare.

From *The Kids of Degrassi Street* and *Degrassi Junior High* in the '80s, to *Degrassi High*, the series was airing in over 140 countries. The newest incarnation, *Degrassi: The Next Generation*, was likely to be just as popular. The series had become a part of the global youth zeitgeist, attracting the devotion of such pop culture influencers as screenwriter/director/actor Kevin Smith, who peppered his own work with references to show, and in 2005 went on to guest star in a few episodes of the new series.

For Drake, the chance to audition for one of the most successfully branded Canadian teen TV shows of all time meant he had to bring his A-game. Interestingly, for the first time in his life, Drake pulled a Snoop and brought his Mary Jane game to the audition too. "I had actually smoked marijuana for the first time, before I went to the audition," he admitted in a 2009 NARAS event interview. "So, it was going to be fun." It was a surprising risk to take — perhaps due to a bad combination of nerves and teen angst — but Drake said that it made him "a little looser." But how exactly did he keep his illicit tokes under wraps? "I was in the bathroom splashing water on my face," he said.

After an exhaustive audition process, Drake was cast. "Apparently they had been auditioning for *Degrassi* for a whole year or something, at all these schools in the city, and it was the last three weeks of auditions, and he got in," explained his mom. When his mom first got the news, she was excited. "I called Aubrey and I asked him to come home because we lived right across the street from the school at the time, and he came home, and then I told him, and he of course went crazy, he couldn't believe it."

Degrassi co-creator Linda Schuyler ultimately made the decision to first cast him at 13 years old. Schuyler reflected on that spark that Drake exhibited at a young age, despite not having any significant acting experience. Schuyler told the *Toronto Star* that Drake was "very charismatic, even as a rather awkward 13 year old when he started here. He had a way of connecting with people." Originally the role that he auditioned for was to play a Greek football player. "We were looking for an athletic, friend-of-everybody type," Schuyler said. "Aubrey had a charm about him, and a warmth, that same beautiful smile he has now. He was green as anything, but willing to do whatever it takes." After seeing his immense potential, the *Degrassi* creators changed the white football player role into the character of the black basketball player he became known for — Jimmy Brooks. "It's what I auditioned for, and they just changed the role. And then came Jimmy Brooks, this character that they almost made as I walked in there, which was a great feeling. It let me know that I impressed them. It was cool to be a part of something from the jump, the first episode, the first day of shooting I was there."

While the steady work and handsome paycheck that came with *Degrassi* was good, Drake was anxious for other work opportunities. Often they were only bit roles, like his appearance on drama *Soul Food* or Canadian crime drama *Blue Murder*. In 2002 he landed a guest spot on TV movie *Conviction*, starring Omar Epps and Dana Delany. It was a small part, but the experience of acting alongside Omar Epps was worth more than his actual screen time. "To work with him was amazing, because as a young black man, [I realized] we have many talented people, and Omar Epps is definitely one of them," he told the *Canadian Jewish News*.

Even as a new actor, Drake had the confidence that fans see in him today as a chart-topping rapper, exhibiting a maturity and composure that belied his years. The producers and story editors at *Degrassi* were duly impressed by his work ethic and charisma. "Aubrey is a total character, you see him strut into the building, and his walk, his demeanor, announces that he's here," said Nicole Hamilton, an associate producer at *Degrassi* on *Degrassi Unscripted*. "When you see him, you're like, 'This kid has it together,' and you know he's gonna go places," added Shelley Scarrow, an executive story editor. "He's got charm just trailing behind him on the floor, and you can see that onscreen but I think he's got even more in real life, which is scary."

Doing whatever it took to make it in his young career meant enduring grueling workdays that he had not been accustomed to. For full-day shoots, Drake would rise at 5 a.m. to get ready for work, beginning his workday at 6 a.m., and running all the way until 8 p.m. Drake described marathon days on set: "It's hard work. People think it's easy. To be on your feet and having people tugging and pulling you, saying, 'You're done this scene, now come over here and do this interview. Now come over here and talk to these fans and take this picture. Now you're going back to work — you're going to block shoot, and rehearse this, and the director wants to talk to you. Here's your lines for the next scene.' It's really overwhelming. You gotta be rested, and if you're not, it's the hardest thing in the world."

But his hard work was paying off as accolades started pouring in. In 2002, he shared the Young Artist Award for Best Ensemble in a TV series for his work on *Degrassi*, and by 2004 he'd earn a nomination all his own for Best Supporting Actor in a TV series. However, like many young TV stars, Drake's social life was quite different from the norm. While some of his friends and peers were focused on living typical teen lifestyles, playing a typical teen on TV meant Drake didn't have time for that. He left Forest Hill Collegiate and switched to Vaughan Road Academy, enrolling in the INTERACT program, a flexible schooling option for high school students who are heavily involved in the arts or athletics program outside of school.

His love life, too, was mostly lived out onscreen. In the first season, Jimmy's relationship with Paige — a girl he had been courting as part of the storyline — was getting quite steamy. "One of the first scenes we ever had together at the very beginning, like in first season, was when we had to kiss, and I remember it was so awkward," confessed actor Lauren Collins, who played Paige. But once they locked lips the sparks between the two characters flew as their scripts said they should. "I think as a kisser Aubrey's an 11 out of 10," said Collins of the first time they kissed onscreen. "Even though it was like two seconds long . . . he comes off very smooth and suave, which he is."

Drake, for his part, was lapping it all up. "I always enjoy the kissing scenes," admitted Drake. "I'm like, yeah, I get to get a little action there, it comes with the job, man, I love it, it's great." Drake also got along with cast members he wasn't smooching, notably Shane Kippel, who played the role of Spinner, Jimmy's best friend on the show. "Out of anybody on set, I'd say that me and Shane had good chemistry. . . . It's way too many jokes going on, we're completely unprofessional, but it comes across onscreen as natural," Drake remarked. Likewise, Kippel also greatly admired the impressive onscreen chemistry they both had: "There's not one thing I don't like about him, we've never had any issues, we've always been completely open with each other. . . . I don't know, there's something about him that you'll just fall in love with."

Back offscreen, Drake was happier at Vaughan Road Academy, which offered a welcome change from the homogenous school environment he had grown up in. The latent racism he reportedly experienced socially at Forest Hill formed a part of his decision to go to Vaughan Road Academy, a significantly more culturally diverse school near "Little Jamaica." Only a highway, the Allen

Expressway, and the Eglinton West subway station separated these two worlds of kosher and curry. His new environment made him feel more at home, but it also exposed him to new cultural and musical inspirations. "When I first started to rap was when I went to this new school, complete other side of the spectrum," he said. "This was in a predominantly Jamaican side of town, and the school had a reputation of being tough, and it was better to deal with than what I was dealing with before."

Meanwhile, on *Degrassi*, his character Jimmy turned to rap music as a way of expressing his emotions, just like Aubrey Graham did in real life. While Drake had dabbled in hip hop before, his new classmates pushed him to take it to the next level. "I was friends with this kid that would put you on the spot all the time. I guess he read my rhyme books at my house and one day he just put me on blast at school," explained Drake. "He told this kid I wanted to battle him and it became this big thing. So I went home and wrote all these rhymes for him — yeah, I cheated — came to school the next day and killed the guy. From there I just started getting into rapping and becoming comfortable with myself."

Despite fitting in better at Vaughan Road, school just never quite seemed to be Drake's forte. He reflected, "I had a difficult time in high school, as a student, I really wasn't the best student in school." One day in history class he began arguing with his teacher and he stood up and grabbed his backpack as if to leave. "He was like, 'If you do . . . And I never came back." Drake was officially a high school dropout.

Looking back, he explained, "It's not something that I'm proud of, but it was definitely a decision I don't regret." Given that his mother was an educator, she was upset with him at the time, especially since he had been so close to finishing high school. As a concession to his mom, whom he cherishes so deeply, Drake said, "One day maybe I will take a break and get the credits, just to be able to hand her a diploma and say, 'I did it for you.'" In the summer of 2012, Drake said he was working on getting his last high school credit.

By the fourth season, it was becoming quite clear that Jimmy was becoming one of the more popular characters on the show, so the writers decided to have his character play a central role in arguably one of the most explosive scenes in the show's history. When Rick, a

The cast of *Degrassi: The Next Generation* with character Jimmy Brooks (a.k.a. Drake) in his wheelchair (© CTV Television Network via PhotoFest)

perpetually harassed classmate, returns to school after having served a long suspension, Jimmy joins in with the others in picking up where they left off, bullying Rick mercilessly. While Jimmy decides to back off after a while, the others play a *Carrie*-like prank on Rick, making him believe he wins a game show, only to dump paint and feathers on him. Rick's finally pushed too far, and he returns to the school with a gun and shoots, leaving Jimmy a paraplegic.

Growing up able-bodied, Drake had to dig a bit deeper to explore this new side of his character. Intent on going the extra mile, Drake said, "I actually took a kid who was in a wheelchair out. I tried to understand how difficult it is to be mobile and live life as if nothing is wrong." The experience left an impression on the young, able-bodied actor, inspiring him to take his acting to the next level. "Just being around people who are in that similar situation and just seeing how life changes, that's a very real emotion when your world comes crashing down and you're changed permanently. . . . It takes a lot of work to capture that emotion." Even when he wasn't filming, Drake would wheel around on set with a lightweight titanium wheelchair. He got so good at navigating the wheelchair, some of the cast and crew on set called him "Mr. Mobility" or "Wheelchair Jimmy." Transforming himself into Jimmy Brooks for hours on end awakened Aubrey to the plight of the disabled and helped him look at his own life with new gratitude. "Playing Jimmy all day and being able to get up and walk away is weird; I appreciate things a lot more now," he said.

Degrassi Executive Producer Aaron Martin explained how Drake ended up playing a central role in what is widely considered to be one of the most cataclysmic scenes in the TV show's history. "After three seasons of seeing what an amazing job Aubrey could do, we realized that in the fourth season he needed his own big storyline," said Martin. "The great thing about Aubrey is that Aubrey never plays it like a victim. Aubrey I don't think ever could play it as a victim, because Aubrey's way too full of life."

In 2005, *Degrassi* became popular enough in the U.S. that the cast did a series of mall tours to greet die-hard fans ("There are very few subtle *Degrassi* fans," Drake said). "We would get 3,000 or 4,000 kids," said *Degrassi* co-creator Schuyler. "And Aubrey even then had this aura about him as a rock star."

Drake's newfound Canadian celeb status couldn't have come at a better time, just as the actor was trying to get serious about his music career. He had begun to upload more songs he had recorded onto Myspace (the most popular place for musicians to share their work at the time). His page became a destination for *Degrassi* fans who were curious about his music creations, and his friend list began growing by the hundreds, then thousands. Was his rapid accumulation of "friends" a result of the high quality of his music? Perhaps, but certainly his music wouldn't have reached so many ears and found so many passionate advocates without the help of his alter-ego Jimmy. But if it was Jimmy who brought them to the site, it was Drake who kept them there. Acting and rapping are two radically different skill sets, and there are a bunch of actors who rap lousily (Joaquin Phoenix, Brian Austin Green), as there are rappers who act terribly (DMX, Method Man). Luckily Drake managed to excel at both. And his preternatural boy-next-door good looks didn't hurt with female fans either.

His own lyrics and delivery aside, Drake had the benefit of working with producer Matthew "Boi-1da" Samuels, who was winning local area Battle of the Beatmakers competitions for producers. Since the digital download boom, albums didn't pay the bills, and the biggest moneymaker was playing live shows at whatever venues were available. Musicians now focus less on selling CDs than they do on building online relationships. Thanks to *Degrassi*, Drake had a built-in audience who would come out to see him perform or just to shake his hand.

Drake didn't deny the leg up he got from being a teen TV star, but he also knew the importance of reaching out to that fanbase.

"The show is definitely the reason I can go to L.A. and go to mall tours and they're sold out. At the end of the day we have a fanbase off the show," conceded Drake. "A lot of artists just have Myspace, and just have a couple songs but don't have a website, don't have marketing, don't have anything, and then they get disappointed when they only sell 70 records. You gotta understand that this whole thing is about marketing, it's about your image, it's about your story, you gotta be appealing to people, and if you're gonna release a record in Canada, you have to do something that nobody else has done or there's no point."

Part of Drake's marketing strategy was self-releasing mixtape songs over the internet. He reportedly used some of his *Degrassi* dough, and money borrowed from his uncle, to help bankroll his rap dreams. The actor-cum-rapper released his first mixtape, *Room for Improvement*, in February 2006. While mixtape culture has been around since 1970 technically, it's been popularized in modern times by hip hoppers like 50 Cent and Lil Wayne, who frequently released new downloads. These mixtapes might contain collaborations, remixes, freestyles and voice-overs, reusing previously heard instrumental tracks from other artists. It's a sure-fire way to keep a musician's street buzz alive while devoted fans wait for their next proper release. For example, 50 Cent owes his early rise to his *Power of the Dollar* mixtape, a widely bootlegged album released in 2000 that caught the ear of Eminem, who then guided 50's development. Drake seemed to have a similar strategy in mind.

Offline Drake was already handing out CDs on the *Degrassi* set. The cast and crew were starting to embrace and appreciate his talent, and nudged him into sliding some samples of his music over to the show's co-creator Linda Schuyler. The early thinking was that if the show's producers liked his music, maybe they might feature it on the show. Executive producer Linda Schuyler, series producer Stefan Brogren (who played Snake in *Degrassi Junior High* and *The Next Generation*) and *Degrassi*'s screenwriters were impressed by his music skills. Schuyler reported, "The writers say his lyrics are eloquent, clear, honest and he's going through a lot of genuine self-examination." Added Brogren, "I find his lyrics really truthful about who he is, the darker side, though. He's half-black, half-Jewish, with a white mom — so many different backgrounds that he maybe never felt accepted in certain circles. It would feel false if he was talking about gangbanging, but he raps about his experience."

According to Schuyler, Drake was a bit hesitant to share his rap songs with his bosses: "He said, 'I do some swearing on it and I don't know if I want Linda to hear it.' Which is so cute." The other problem with bringing his music to the show, said Brogren, was that Drake didn't think his character Jimmy would be given the opportunity to rap. During Drake's final season on *Degrassi* in 2009, the producers turned his character into a rapper allegedly against his wishes. "I was really apprehensive about it because this is my whole leap from [*Degrassi*] and now you're going to make me into a rapper character?" he said. "So I wrote my own verses and tried to keep it as not-corny as possible. And it worked out."

Brogren didn't feel it necessary to have genuine high level hip hop rotating on the show, just something that was hip hoppy and carried the infectious energies of the genre. "We said, 'Whatever rap you do it doesn't have to be Drake-level hip hop. In fact, it needs to be less.' He did do it in the end. And I think he was happy." It's a testament to Drake's abilities that he could write and perform the songs not from his own point of view, but from his character's — a feat that merged his acting experience with his developing songwriting skills. Said Drake, "I think it was beneficial being an actor first. It taught me about being poised, about having class, how to deal with interviews and fans."

While Drake's acting career on the show seemed to be going well — he'd even appeared in the 2008 special *Degrassi Spring Break Movie* — the show was about to go through some major changes, unbeknownst to him. Allegedly without any forewarning from the show's producers, the cast was going to be re-tooled — and Jimmy Brooks no longer had a place on the show. Drake had starred on the show for seven years starting in 2001, but when his character "graduated" from *Degrassi* in 2009 his days at Degrassi Community School would be over. He appeared in 138 episodes in total.

But you can't play a teen forever, nor would Drake want to. When asked by a *Notable Interviews* reporter whether he felt his *Degrassi* days were numbered, he replied, "They would never be numbered because of my age [21], they would be numbered because I'm just done with it. I'm sure *Degrassi* as a show would love for me to stay forever, they'd love to be renewed forever because that's money and they'd love to keep making episodes forever."

Though fans were sorry to see Drake go, he left behind a significant *Degrassi* legacy. He'd played a big part in one of the most dramatic moments in the show's history, and his character's relationship with Hazel was *TNG*'s second longest, lasting nearly two years. (The longest-lasting relationship in the history of the show at the time was between Toby and Kendra, and it lasted two years.) But then before he knew it, it appeared that he was getting too old to be that same child actor. He pursued other acting opportunities over the next year, appearing on CBC shows like *Being Erica*, *Sophie* and *The Border*, but he wasn't finding any work that extended beyond a one-episode stint.

It was a good time to leave his comfort zone and follow a new direction. "A lot of it's dependent on music, if my music takes off. *Degrassi* has been a great stepping stone, but I'd like to move into movies and bigger projects. I'm kinda apprehensive about staying on a series because usually actors from a series never really get to do much afterwards, so I'm really looking to make that leap into movies more." But even as he dreamed big, Drake stayed realistic. Without a steady source of income, and not yet making significant money as a rapper, he was on the verge of looking for a day job. "I was coming to terms with the fact that, okay, people know me from *Degrassi*, but I might have to work at a restaurant or something just to keep things going," he said.

Drake wanted to do the music thing, but he also wanted to continue to work as an actor. It's what he knew. In Drake's mother's basement where he used to live and record his early works lies a letter sent from a fan of his, a letter that he describes as "one of the nicest letters I've ever received from anybody." In the letter the ardent fan says that Drake has the opportunity to become one of the greatest black actors the world has ever seen. "He feels that I can complete the trifecta of the greatest African-American actors of all time," said Drake. "Sidney Poitier, Denzel Washington, and he says the third addition would be Aubrey Graham. . . . I will keep it with me for the rest of my life . . . if it happens, it happens."

DRIZZY 2.0:

New Millennial Emcee

In the late '90s, Public Enemy's Chuck D presciently spoke of a day when bricks-and-mortar multi-national record companies would have much less relevance in musicians' lives, and experimented with having his fans buy his music directly from his own web-based record label SLAMjamz. While these moves were greeted with mixed reviews at the time, he was arguably far ahead of his time. Today musicians utilize all kinds of DIY music-sharing approaches: free downloads, pay-what-you-can models or smart sample-before-you-pay music sites. The hugely popular Bandcamp.com allows musicians to sell their music and merchandise directly to their fans, taking a minimal cut of sales from the site, ranging from a 10 to 15 percent commission.

Drake became one of the poster children for this Brave New World of music production and distribution, a world where blogs, Twitter followers and music streamed directly via artists' websites can make or break a career. One might argue being based in Canada gave Drake an advantage, in that his home country has consistently ranked at or near the top of worldwide internet engagement for the last decade. According to web research firm comScore, Canadians spend almost twice the amount of time online than the worldwide average (43.5 hours a month versus 23.1 hours). This, coupled with the fact that Canada is largely viewed as a file-sharing haven due to less rigid copyright laws, created basic conditions for Drake to release a bevy of rap music online to build his brand. As a millennial, going to the internet was certainly a natural way to reach out to his intended audience: social media use amongst teens and 20-somethings rates higher than the Gen X or baby boomer population. Interestingly, Drake's racial profile may have been a factor in his strong adoption of online media as well. For example, blacks disproportionately tweet more. According to Pew Research Centre surveys, by May 2011, 25 percent of online African-Americans were using Twitter, compared with only 9 percent for whites, while one in ten African-American internet users visit Twitter on a typical day, which is nearly four times the rate for whites.

Whatever the conditions that led him to the opportunities the internet had to offer, Drake used these online tools to their full potential. In addition to releasing music on Myspace, Drake later took advantage of free blog hosting with the October's Very Own blog (octobersveryown.blogspot.ca), named after the fact that he and many of his friends were born in October. Like Myspace, and later Twitter, it was a way to connect directly with fans, strengthening relationships with old fans and attracting new ones. Drake knew that his heavily digitized bottom-up distribution was the wave of the future, and hosting it from his own site gave him more control than ever.

While Prince first championed this idea of getting one's music directly to the fans digitally through his website subscription service (now called NPGMusicClub.com), and Radiohead further fine-tuned this concept, they were already very successful signed artists with dedicated audiences. *Then* they decided to invert the music industry pyramid. While Drake had a fanbase, they weren't necessarily just fans of his music, nor CD-buying, concert-going diehards. He had to entice them to follow him into a whole new field.

It was a fellow burgeoning rapper from Toronto named Promise who introduced Drake to the magic of Myspace, and building one's social media clout, to increase his cred in the Toronto rap scene. Promise, whose 2011 *Awakening* CD boasts recording credits from Kanye West's cousin the World Famous Tony Williams and production by 9th Wonder's Soul Council, had developed a great reputation in local music circles for his DIY approach to music and gave Drake some of his first real studio recording experiences. It is believed that he was courted by his current label Duck Down Music, a legendary hip hop record label, partly because he was savvy enough as a truly independent DIY artist to score collaborations with A-list urban acts like Slum Village and Royce da 5'9". A mutual friend, singer/songwriter Jermaine "Jai" Brown, brought Drake and Promise together. Brown, according to Promise, told Drake "he should check me out and that I was dope and he'd like it." He recalled, "When we first met on the set of *Degrassi*, he had said he was just writing a bunch of songs and not really recording, but he wanted to, which led to me bringing him to my spot, and we just started bangin' joints out both for his solo stuff and mine." Though some would dismiss Drake as a pseudo-famous rap wannabe, his skills were enough to convince Promise he could be the real deal. "I was amazed at how well he wrote for someone who wasn't actually an artist. So I encouraged him to keep writing and invited him to my studio, where he recorded his first hits that later ended up on his *Room for Improvement* mixtape.

Toronto rap scenesters can be hard on their own. Some of this attitude comes from being based in a city where American music imperialism overwhelms indigenous music productions, and where historically few urban music practitioners get genuine mainstream industry supports, concert bookings, label interest or any of the same opportunities afforded their indie rock counterparts. It creates a crabs-in-the-barrel effect, and the reception to Drake's early music was no different. Said Promise, "I remember trying to put him on to a lot of people in our city but they all brushed me off like, 'That kid from *Degrassi*!? C'mon, Prom!,' completely discrediting the fact that he was a dope writer with a smooth flow, clean image, media training and a large fanbase."

If Promise didn't nudge Drake to experiment with Myspace, the social media–infused Drake narrative might have altogether been a different story. "[Promise] was like, 'Yo, get a Myspace, it's the new thing,' and I didn't even know what it was," admitted Drake. "[Promise] would be like, 'It's the new thing, you'll do so well on there, it gets your music out,' and I kept ignoring his invite request, and then eventually everything was just Myspace, Myspace, Myspace." Why did Promise share his trade secrets? "I saw the advantage he already had being a young actor. His fanbase was massive so I showed him how it would benefit him in the future when he started to put stuff out," said Promise, who recorded an unreleased joint project with Drake called DRPR. "It's funny, 'cause at first he was brushing Myspace off, but it helped jump-start his career."

It was clear to Drake that he now needed to translate his Myspace cachet into cash. His rapid social media climb had generated some buzz, but he was still coming from a country that is better known for exporting comedians (Jim Carrey, Mike Myers, Russell Peters, Tom Green, Michael Cera) than it was for any rappers. And there was no defined path for him to follow, because few

Toronto rappers had even come close to breaking out in America before him. Especially not in the digital era.

Regardless, music industry gatekeepers were forced to take notice of this slick, young rapper. And his camp did their best to make sure that the industry did take notice. In the digital age, A&R reps were only an email away, and in 2006, when Drake was about to launch his first mixtape, his camp sent an email letter to a large group of major record label executives and A&Rs of note, including esteemed figures like L.A. Reid and Doug Morris. The letter was sent out on behalf of a sports and entertainment finance group called Frozen Moments out of Philadelphia. This dubious email boasted that Drake's music was "a blend of Common and Jay-Z," that he was not "just another pretty face," that he was recording "songs best understood by a genuine hustler" and came replete with quotes from director Kevin Smith on what a great actor he was ("Drake is the finest in our cast — one of the greatest performers I've seen"). This correspondence, which listed a Hotmail contact address and was ridden with typos (it called him a "bonified hottie"), might have demonstrated his camp's naïveté, but such a bold move couldn't help but highlight his confidence and determination to succeed.

By February 14, 2006, he released his first recorded mixtape for sale, *Room for Improvement*, a 22-track playlist of unlicensed songs with 17 original tracks and a few remixes. It was hosted by Florida's DJ Smallz, who had become popular in the hip hop world because of his *Southern Smoke* mixtape series. Smallz had built up a respectable portfolio, having already produced mixtapes with leading rap figures like Lil Wayne and Young Jeezy, so Drake was clearly in high-level company. *Room for Improvement* featured a mishmash of high-profile rappers like Lupe Fiasco and Clipse, and other more obscure regional southern talents like Nickelus F. Along with an overwhelming list of American talents, like Harlem's Nick Rashur and D.C.'s DJ Ra, Drake made sure to bring along a motley crew of burgeoning Toronto-based talents on his first real introduction to the wider rap universe.

Amir, a Persian-Canadian emcee and producer, who came to Canada in 1987 from Iran, is credited with producing five of the songs on *Room for Improvement.* He first started working with Drake while he was still a teen haunting the halls of Degrassi Community School. "When we first exchanged info and he sent me songs, I didn't even know he was on TV at that time. From the time I heard he was that young, and heard his skills, I knew the kid was dope. He was ahead of kids that age, like when your typical 15- or 16-year-old picks up the mic, and flows, rhymes and talks about the type of stuff he was talking about, it was real hip hop, real lyrical."

As a producer, taking on the "*Degrassi* Rap Guy" as a client was not exactly considered a career booster. "I think some people had a problem with him, feeling that he was corny or something, in their eyes," admitted Amir. "There was many people in the industry, no need to name names, when I told them about Aubrey at that time, many people laughed in my face, man. No word of a lie. And some of those same people are the biggest bandwagon riders now. You can't blame people for not having the foresight. Canadian hip hop had never gone far historically, so it's hard to have that big vision when it's never happened before."

Fellow Toronto-area beatsmith Slakah the Beatchild, who Drake tweeted in January 2012 as "one of my favorite producers I ever worked with," also worked on a number of songs on *Room for Improvement* including "Bad Meaning Good," "Thrill Is Gone" and "Make Things Right." He opened up his Scarborough-area studio to the young wordsmith because of his relentless work ethic. "He was doing *Degrassi* at the time, so he'd usually come by the studio after shooting on set," explained Slakah, whose groundbreaking 2008 *Soul Movement Vol. 1* release on the influential BBE label featured Drake on a number of his songs.

"We'd just spend the entire night until the sun comes up, working on songs. Sometimes it'd be, nothing would get done, and we'd just be kicking it, going over music, and then a lot of great songs came from that." During the creation of "Thrill Is Gone" in particular, Slakah, who'd produced the beat and created the hook for the song, knew a young Drake was onto something. "I'd given an artist [Promise] a beat tape, and he passed that to Drake. And Drake heard a beat on there, loved it, and recorded something on there. . . . When he sent me back what he recorded, I knew right away. I was like, 'This is amazing.' I knew he was going to blow up." Slakah later told the *Toronto Star*, "Within the music community, we all said Drake was going to be the next [rap superstar] . . . with his wordplay and understanding of metaphors, he'd be a great English professor. He can say something 10 different ways and make it rhyme."

Amir similarly recalls Drake's stellar early work ethic while recording "Try Harder" and "A Scorpio's Mind" on *Room for Improvement*. "To create 'Try Harder' we used to have these MSN sessions, into the wee hours of the night. You're talking like at 2 a.m., he'd say, 'I have a sample, you think you could work with this?' and I would try to chop it up on the spot, send it back to him, staying up from 1 a.m. to 6 a.m.! Exchanging ideas, beats and rhymes back and forth. He told me he wanted hard-hitting drums, sample-driven beats at that time."

While recording "A Scorpio's Mind," a song Amir calls "one of my favorite tracks I've done with him," he saw Drake's songwriting talent begin to emerge. "I made the beat one week before sharing the beat with Drake at that time," said Amir, who cut his production teeth using old-school Cool Edit Pro programs. "He just liked it, that hip hop groove, old school, with a little bit of guitar lick, which carried that vibe that he was looking for at that time. He took a few days to think on it, and by the time he had come down to record it, he had gotten Nick Fury [a.k.a. Nickelus F, a former Freestyle Friday rap champion on BET] on it. It was really heartfelt. He was really a stay true to yourself type of guy. He was never really stretching too hard to be someone he wasn't."

Voyce Alexander, an emerging R&B pop singer, was featured as a vocalist on a number of the buzzy songs on *Room for Improvement*. Voyce had enjoyed a long history working with Drake, through his creative collaborations with Promise, who had put him on to Drake, so he knew what made Drake tick and how to get the best out of him.

"When I first heard Aubrey it was funny. I grew up in church, so I knew a guy named Promise, and I was sitting in Promise's basement, 'cause that's where we started out doing music together. We were in a group, and this kid was leaving these voicemails on his phone," said Voyce, who has writing credits on "Dem Haters" from Rihanna's sophomore *A Girl Like Me* disc. "And one day Promise messed up and played me one of these voicemails, and it was this incredible kid. I was immediately struck by him, the amount of talent this kid had. And it was Drake on the voicemail. From there Drake asked me if I could do a couple of hooks for him. I'd never met him, but I said yes and we agreed to meet. I said it would be $300 a hook, and how I met him was when he came to bring me the money."

The two became friends outside the studio, with Drake often driving up to see Voyce in Ajax, where the two would just talk about music at the local neighborhood Applebee's for hours. Voyce was more intrigued than anything about the fact that Drake, as a young teenager, always had it in his mind that he wanted to be a rap star, *Degrassi* fame notwithstanding. "We did a song called 'Rewind' — he was in *Degrassi* at this time — and his swag was incredible," said Voyce, who had just graduated from high school in 2003 at the time he started working with Drake, years before he was ready to release a full mixtape. Comparable to a Bruce Banner–Hulk effect, Voyce recalled, "When he started rapping he was a totally different dude. He was so dope to me, still is."

Voyce explained that despite him being a bona fide teen drama TV star, Drake wanted more. "I remember we used to go out some times and people would recognize him, and it was like, 'This guy is a real celebrity.' I never really watched *Degrassi*, didn't know how big the show was, but everywhere we went people were freaking out. He expressed to me a lot how much he hated working there. He hated it: he wanted to be a rap star. He made no bones about it, 'I want to be a rap celebrity . . . this *Degrassi* stuff ain't cutting it for me, I want it all.'"

While years later the two would have some miscommunication issues that culminated in Drake releasing "Exposed," a ruthless diss song about Voyce, Voyce claimed he has no issues with Drake: "I know who he is, he's a really nice guy, a good guy, and I'm very happy for him." The R&B crooner is satisfied that he got to witness Drake's early rap career and contribute to some of the great songs on Drake's debut mixtape. You can hear him singing the hook on the "All This Love" remix. Said Voyce, "I remember one night, Boi-1da was working on some beats, and I was like, 'Yo, Drake, I don't know what you're doing, but you have to come to the studio right now. You would kill this beat.' It was the beat from 'Do What You Do.' When he was rapping, I was like, 'You need to come up with a hook.' I was proud to say I got to drop a line on the Drake record, because he doesn't need anybody to drop a line on his records, because he's got lyrics. But I actually remember giving my two cents and he took it, out of respect, and did it, and it was great."

While *Room for Improvement*, was by no stretch Drake's best work — sonically and lyrically there was indeed some room for improvement — it still generated modest sales with over 6,000 copies sold.

By 2007, the reality of the North American rap game was still one in which most rappers looking to truly make it would have to be able to tap into the U.S. hip hop market, where most of the credible rap media, rap stars and hip hop culture influencers resided. While Drake's team's DIY mandate was simple and reasonably successful, they would need a more insider-based strategy to attack the U.S. rap scene more aggressively.

Some of Drake's crucial U.S. marketplace career navigations would be led by one of America's own rising hot urban music entrepreneurs, Terral "Hollaback" T. Slack, a Lousiana-bred tastemaker who had started out his own company, BPE (Bigger Picture Entertainment), in 2002. When he first heard *Room for Improvement*, the release from the Canadian *Degrassi* kid, he "laughed it off." But the more he listened, the more he saw a kid who had immense potential. "One day I really took time to listen to *Room for Improvement*, and I fell in love with it," said T. Slack. *Room for Improvement* mixtape host DJ Smallz's assistant Jessica linked Drake to Slack, and they hit it off. Slack was anxious to see what Drake's future plans would be. "When I spoke to Drake for the first time, we had a good conversation," he recalled. "I asked if he had management and what he was looking for, and at the time he didn't have anybody in the States. He was looking for management, and wanted somebody to prove themselves."

A clear visionary from the time he started his rap career, Drake laid out a blueprint for Slack. "He painted this whole picture of who he wanted to work with, and who he looked up to, and I basically told him that I had connections to all those people and can make it happen," recalled Slack. Making key connections to America's urban music elite oftentimes means an artist needs deep enough pockets to be able to afford guest artists on their mixtapes. Because Drake had already been a gainfully employed teen TV star, that wasn't really an issue. Said Slack, " [Drake] let me know what his budget was, and when I first met Drake he funded everything himself. He used his *Degrassi* money to fund all his projects. He went to work basically to pay for his rap career."

Though Slack had major U.S. connections, he also saw the value of strengthening connections with Drake's fans — and that meant going back to Myspace. The manager took charge and decided that if more attention was paid to the day-to-day management of Drake's Myspace account, he could easily quadruple his online fanbase. "Drake had so many fans bombard him, but he really didn't have time to hit everybody back," explained Slack. "So what I did, I brought him my team, my assistant Kryshane Lee and my brother Eric, who's a lawyer, and I basically had my team reply back to all of his fans, and they were blown away: 'Oh my God, Drake just replied back to me.'" Before Drake, Slack and his team knew it, the budding rapper had become one of the rap kings of Myspace. "Before I stepped in, Drake probably had 20,000– 30,000 fans back when Myspace was popping, then when I stepped in and did my thing, it quickly reached one million."

Drake with music impresario T. Slack, who played a key role in Drake's early success (© Rob Lee)

It was an unheard-of feat, and the music industry was buzzing. For good reason: in 2007, Myspace ranked Drake the most popular unsigned Canadian artist. Slack's social media masterplan was multi-layered: "It was a couple different fan pages that we made for him at the time. Like, we had Drake Canada, Drake U.S. — we kinda built up a whole brand for him that basically touched every fan. I built a 'Talk to Drake' email where fans could actually talk to him. . . . The fans really wanted to touch him, and that's basically what I did, I tried to touch every fan and reach out to 'em." Slack even updated the songs available on Drake's page based on fan feedback. His team also achieved a major coup when they landed Drake prime time media exposure on Sirius Satellite's *Shade 45* morning show, and in major hip hop publications like *XXL* and the *Source*.

With this media recognition and Slack's connections, Drake could now seek out collaborations with A-list American urban music artists he liked for his next mixtape, 2007's *Comeback Season*. His target: Trey Songz. Songz was a bubbling R&B talent who had all the tools to make it: a great silky smooth voice and drop-dead

45

good looks. After being featured on a single from popular Chicago rapper Twista's fifth album, *The Day After* ("Girl Tonite" charted as high as #3 on the *Billboard* R&B/Hip Hop Songs chart), Songz's star began to rise. Quickly.

How could a lesser-known rapper from an obscure city (in the urban music context, at least) get to record with a credible R&B singer who might feel he has little to gain from a collaboration? It was time for Slack to work some managerial magic, while Drake did the additional artistic selling. While driving with his friends Dio and Niko to Waterloo, Ontario, to visit fellow rapper JD Era, Drake was playing this beat over and over again, and started writing the hook. And then he had an epiphany. "I gotta get Trey on this," he said. He called up Slack. Slack then got Delonte Murphy, an affiliate of Trey Songz, on the phone, and the next thing he knew, Trey got a copy of Drake's incomplete song. It was good enough for Trey to invite the Canuck rapper out to Atlanta to work on some music, and they hit it off immediately. Recalled Drake, "When I got there he told me, 'I don't just jump on any record, I turn down a lot of people. A lot of people want me on their songs, but the songs are just not up to par: I don't do it, even if they have the money.'"

Slack recounted this crucial connection that he says he helped set up, one that would change Drake's career forever: "Drake went to Trey's manager's house at the time, the home studio, and Trey actually cut the record in the basement. Trey knocked it out in probably 15 minutes . . . and Drake paid for that out of his own pocket. The record was already partially done, Trey just added on the ending and part of the hook."

After hanging out, they both realized that though they had different styles and talents, they were a great complement to one another's careers. "I love R&B, but I can't do it as well as he can," admitted Drake. "He is one of the best singers I've ever heard in my life, and I think he's vice versa: he loves rap, and I think he admires what I'm able to do with a rap verse. So me and Trey just saw eye to eye, just being two young dudes who have the same interests — females, music, money. We just bonded."

The result of their shared music interest was the smooth R&B–heavy rap song "Replacement Girl" for *Comeback Season*. Collaborating with the driven young emcee reminded Trey of his own early career struggles, so he lent Drake a hand outside of the recording studio too: he referenced their "Replacement Girl" song on his own Myspace page. The track became an instant web phenomenon.

Between Drake's growth as a rapper and the support of stars like Trey, the stage was set for *Comeback Season* to really catch the ear of the North American urban music elite. The mixtape (and Slack's connections) also attracted A-list American guest artists like Detroit-bred Dwele, a Grammy-nominated vocalist who is now famously known for having been featured on the first single, "Power," of Kanye West's groundbreaking *My Beautiful Dark Twisted Fantasy*.

Dwele broke down how the buzzy track "Don't You Have a Man" (which also featured Little Brother) came about: "My manager, Ron Estill, connected me to his manager at the time, T. Slack, and I actually didn't work in the same studio with him on that song. That was one of those situations where we took advantage of technology, and he got the track together and sent it out to me, and I just cut it at my in-house studio in Detroit, and I really liked how it came together. The hook and everything was already written, all he really used me for was my instrument, my voice. The concept, the lyrics, pretty much everything was already done with that one."

Comeback Season wasn't guested entirely by American A-listers; Drake also enlisted some of his hometown's finest talents. Burgeoning beatsmith Ritchie "Rich Kidd" Acheampong, who is credited with producing the first full song on *Comeback Season*, in addition to a few others like "Faded" and "Easy to Please," first got connected to Drake through rising Lebanese-Canadian producer Noah "40" Shebib. 40 was teaching Rich Kidd to mix at influential

Drake and Trey Songz flank BET's Stephen Hill
(© Adrian Sidney/PictureGroup)

Toronto urban arts incubator the Remix Project, where youth are taught practical artistic skills that will prepare them for a career. Kidd now boasts production credits from a who's who of Canadian (k-os) and American (Kendrick Lamar) premier rap talents. Said Rich Kidd, "I was already in the Remix Project making beats, and [Drake] would come in the room and be like, 'Yo, that beat is dope, can you put that on a USB stick and bring it to the recording room?'"

The recording sessions took place either within the Remix Project studios and/or at Toronto's Carpet Factory in the west end, on Mowat Avenue. Nickelus F appeared on the original version of the song "Faded," though Kidd believed, "Styles P was supposed to add his verse to that." Other songs produced by Rich Kidd played a key role in how the mixtape would flow track to track. Said Kidd, "The 'Hesitation' song I did at my crib, Drake gave me the Donnell Jones sample to cut up, and I was like, 'I can do it, I can flip anything.' I flipped it up, did a little intro to it, and he was loving it."

One of Rich Kidd's finest achievements as producer on *Comeback Season* involved "The Last Hope," which took off virally "all because of what Drake did with the beat," said Kidd. "I was really surprised at how many people spit on that beat. Somebody looped the beat, put an instrumental on YouTube and everybody went wild on it — Styles P, Drag-On, Ransom — and most recently DMX is rapping on it, and it's on a DJ Khaled mixtape featuring the Ruff Ryders."

Other *Comeback Season* guests like Kardinal Offishall, Toronto's most respected emcee not named Drake, who is featured on "The Last Hope" alongside vocalist Andreena Mill, recalled that it was while recording the song with Drake that he learned about how social media was reshaping the rap industry. "I still remember that night when we were down there in the studio — me, Drake, Saukrates, Solitaire — and we were talking about the different generations, and that's the first time that I realized that there was a thorough difference between how people understood hip hop today," explained Kardinal, who is noted for his distinctive dance hall–reggae influenced rap flows and, most recently, for his smash single "Dangerous" featuring Grammy-nominated Akon. Said Kardinal, "Drake was sharing with us how important it was what was reflected online, on message boards, on blogs. At that time, computer gangsterism and that kind of thing never fazed me even two percent. When we came up, real life people pulled real life guns, or you'd be in the same building as somebody who wanted to do bodily harm to you. The idea of people hiding behind keyboards and having this online community, that was the first time that I got a glimpse into that life." He added, "It was the first time I learned how social media shaped his feelings, how he records material, and shaped the reception of when he comes out."

Rich Kidd echoes similar sentiments regarding Drake's advanced social media awareness. "Producing *Comeback Season*, it wasn't a money thing. I got paid for some of the joints but he sounds dope. When he released it and it was getting all this blog love, this is when I first started learning about blog sites, how people expressed that they are loving the tracks."

When *Comeback Season* came out and Drake became even more popular, he was still greatly misunderstood in his own hometown. "I hang out in the streets, the 'hood, and to them it was like, 'This guy's rapping?'" said Rich Kidd. "There was a lot of hate for what he was doing, because he made this transition from acting on *Degrassi* to trying to spit bars, and the 'hood is always going to look at it like, 'How are you gonna take our art form?' Like these commercial guys, guys from outside the 'hood are using it to big up themselves. People always took that angle when they found out I was doing stuff with Drake. At the end of the day I was like, 'This dude can rap.' He's not talking about guns, selling drugs — he can just rap. At the time I don't think people appreciated what he was trying to do." While the blogs were lighting up with numerous mentions of Drake, it was the old school media world that played an equal, if not greater, part in his ascent. When Drake shot his first independently produced video for "Replacement Girl," the feedback from major video networks like BET was immediate.

While other Canadian rap artists like k-os and Kardinal had gotten their videos some play on BET, America's number one urban video outlet, they had the benefit of major label backing to make that corporate push. On April 30, 2007, Drake's "Replacement Girl" video premiered on BET's *106 & Park*, and he became the first unsigned Canadian rapper to have a debut music video screened on BET in its 27-year history. It would take another four years for any other Canadian independent urban music act to make their mark on the influential show, when Toronto's Linda Luztono was the first unsigned Canadian female artist ever invited to perform.

Reportedly during the filming of the "Replacement Girl" video he would befriend Shebib — nicknamed "40" for his ability to work relentlessly, referencing the 40 days and 40 nights of his biblical namesake — a rising beatsmith who had a good sense for what musical concoctions matched Drake's rhyme flows. The two started to develop a strong friendship that went beyond music. Interestingly, the two had some similar histories. 40, diagnosed with multiple sclerosis in his early 20s (he's attached his name to national Multiple Sclerosis Society campaigns to raise awareness about the disease), was also a fellow former child actor who tried to make a name for himself in the music industry. At the tender age of 10, he played a character named Andrew Winfield in a TV series called *The Mighty Jungle* — which his aunt Suzanna starred in — and would later land a recurring role in the Gemini Award–winning series *Wind at My Back*. By 1999, when he appeared in the critically acclaimed *The Virgin Suicides*, things were starting to look up for the young 40.

Whereas Drake had a strong musical lineage on his American father's side of the family, 40 had equally impressive acting and theater bloodlines in Canada. Both his mother and father made and acted in film, with his dad Donald gaining much notoriety for his 1970 film *Goin' Down the Road*. In fact, 40 says his first time appearing on the big screen was while in his mother Tedde Moore's womb in *A Christmas Story* ("She's got a big belly [in the movie] because it's me.... I'm in that film," he said). His great-grandmother Dora Mavor Moore was a pioneer of Canadian theater, after which a major award — the Canadian equivalent of the Tony Awards — is named. (He even has "Mavor" tattooed on one of his forearms.) But for 40, making it to Hollywood was not to be. After having to overcome obstacles like being robbed at gunpoint and what was described in *Fader* magazine as a "severe run-in with the law for bank fraud" he took the donation that his family doctor provided to purchase recording equipment and to go to music school. He had originally built a reputation in Toronto hip hop circles as DJ Decibel, then started accumulating production credits with respected hardcore Toronto rap collective Empire. "Empire had just got together in 2000," related Adam Bomb, one of the founding group members. "About a year into it, Noah [40], asked someone in the crew if we would come by his spot and check out some of his beats. We came through and ended up doing four or five records. From there on, he was our go-to guy."

Bomb marveled over his uncanny ability to multi-task, engineer songs, work the sound board and produce tracks, skills that are now widely acknowledged as giving Drake a leg up on the music competition, given that 40 is his good friend and right-hand man. "To this day, he is the most efficient and creative person I've ever seen behind the boards," said Bomb. "Things it would take the average engineer 10, 15 minutes to do, 40 could do instantly. We would record and go home thinking the track was complete. On his own time, he would take the vocals and add touch-ups in dozens of spots. Sometimes it was just tightening the ad libs or arranging the beat and the verses differently. Sometimes it was adding effects. Sometimes, he would create an entirely new beat and put the lyrics to it. Usually when a producer does that, the new version doesn't fit as well as the original but when he did it, it not only worked but it was remarkably better." He added, "The funny thing about Noah's beats is that he always had that sound. That '40 sound' behind Drake was always there."

When 40 started working more seriously with Drake on his music, he knew he had inherited a great situation, thanks to his friend's charm and *Degrassi* fanbase. "*Degrassi* was a big part, y'know... it gave us a little bit of an edge from day one," explained 40, who point-blank attributed Drake's early success to his obsessed *Degrassi* fans crossing over with him to the world of urban music. "Where the local rapper from Toronto's Myspace was getting 250 plays a day, Drake's was getting 1,500 from the jump, because of *Degrassi*," he said. But Drake couldn't rest on his Myspace success forever.

Despite "Replacement Girl" putting Drake on the American urban radio and video radar in 2007, Drake felt conflicted about the syrupy image it was sending out to mass audiences. "I'll tell you, I always feel like that was a great song. And at the time, I can't say that it didn't represent me," he said. "It was me at that time. I won't ever say I regret it. I can look back and say, 'Well damn, now that I'm in this position and know this much more, I probably would have done it different.'"

While there was talk on the internet and from Drake himself of a possible collaborative Drake/Trey Songz album that would capture their obvious synergies, it didn't materialize. But even if their musical partnership didn't quite progress, behind the scenes their relationship had. "Trey's been like an older brother to me, he looked out for me, he's the reason my video was on *106 [& Park]*, he's looked out for me in ways that he really didn't have to," said Drake. Had Drake not collaborated with R&B heartthrob Trey Songz on "Replacement Girl" and gotten early tour-date slots with him, it's debatable whether he would have entered the American charts or made it onto BET.

By April 2008, when Myspace was overtaken in popularity by its main competitor, Facebook, it was time for Drake to come up with a new strategy. He decided that he was going to devote more energy to his mixtape releases. Luckily, at his disposal he now had 40, a one-man music production army, a guy who could not only help him interpret his music better than ever, but who also knew how to produce, track, mix and master his songs and could help take Drake to the next level.

WEEZY
AND
DRIZZY

Love Drake or loathe him, it was becoming next to impossible to ignore him, especially if you were employed at a major record label. It wasn't a matter of whether he would get signed, it was a matter of with whom and for how much money. "By me hooking up all of these features for him, it really started to build up the buzz, and that's when we started shopping him," explained T. Slack. "He and his uncle did these press kits and they'd send them to me, and press up these CDs, and I'd just reach out to the connections I had. I reached out to Def Jam, Universal Motown, J Records — everybody."

Record labels were beginning to vie for his attention, and in a *Fader* magazine interview it was revealed that Atlantic Records and Interscope's Jimmy Iovine were in the running to sign him. The Drake camp flew out to the influential Interscope's L.A-based office and had a productive meeting with the label who had monster acts, from Eminem to M.I.A., on their roster. But it just didn't work out. "We went to L.A., met with Manny Smith [A&R] over there, and everybody thought he was dope," explained T. Slack. "They wanted to hear more music, but I didn't have those records that he dropped later on. I just had 'Replacement Girl.' I had great quality records, but I didn't have number one records . . . he had good songs, but they wasn't great songs at the time."

Drake admitted to having record company meetings with Universal Motown, Roc-A-Fella/Def Jam, Koch and Sony/Epic. Mired in mediocre albums and slipping record sales, the labels needed to sign artists with infinite potential to stay in the game. And Drake was the real McCoy, the Real Deal Holyfield. It was alleged that Drake came close to signing with Universal Motown, which was among the larger name record label pursuers.

The stakes were so high that Universal Motown's pursuit of Drake got particularly sticky, with the label's then-president Sylvia Rhone allegedly threatening Drake with legal action to prevent him from signing or dealing with other record labels. "Drake was supposed to sign with Universal Motown: they was real interested," explained T. Slack, in an attempt to illuminate what exactly happened. "We actually flew into New York, and everything was basically good. They was talking about signing the kid, the deal looked like it was about to be bright. We had a meeting with Sylvia and the meeting didn't go too well. Basically in the press kit at the time he had these flashy clothes on, hat to the back, and kinda had swag, he had this perception on the press kit, and he kinda went in the office basic — hoody, jeans — he really didn't have the superstar that you saw in the press kit." They both learned that even talent-focused labels are looking for a certain package. Said T. Slack, "I actually found that out after the meeting … we was all hyped up thinking the meeting was good, and then we'll be in touch, if everything goes good, we wanna fly you up next week, to close the deal, and then we never got the call."

The whole experience with Universal Motown allegedly left a bitter taste in Drake's mouth. Drake dissed Rhone in "Say What's Real." Years later, while accepting his 2011 BMI Songwriter of the Year Award, he took another jab at Rhone, "who told me I didn't have what it took to make it in the music business industry."

The relationship between Drake and T. Slack was getting slightly strained over the pressures for him to live up to the buzz and ink that big deal, among other things. "It was really hard for me to take control of Drake's career because at the time I was still living in Louisiana, small town, and I didn't really have the money to be traveling back and forth," Slack admitted. "I really wasn't around him, and I wanted to but couldn't really move to Toronto at the time and he really couldn't move to the States … that me not being around him kinda took a toll." He added, "A lot of people was in his ear, maybe you should do this, maybe you should do that, it just came to a point where he wanted to better his career." By late 2008 T. Slack was no longer managing Drake, with no deep wounds or hard feelings left from their split. "I much respect him … anytime somebody want to leave the camp to better their situation, to feed their family, I'm all for it, and that's basically what he did."

Luckily Drake's career didn't stall without T. Slack, as he'd connected with someone with even more important industry contacts: rap music's ultimate kingpin, Lil Wayne. A child prodigy who had been rapping professionally since he was nine years old, Wayne had been linked to the influential Cash Money Records label headed up by hip hop impresarios Bryan "Baby" Williams and his brother Ronald "Slim" Williams his whole rap life. By the time he hit his late teens in 1999 he was already a platinum-selling solo artist, with his debut recording, *Tha Block Is Hot*, selling over one million units. Between 2006 and 2007 Wayne utilized the savvy strategy of flooding the marketplace with mixtapes to keep hip hop fans interested until his proper commercial CDs would be released. The quality of his promotional mixtapes was so much better than other artists' official CDs that *Rolling Stone* named two of his mixtapes — *Da Drought 3* and *The Drought Is Over 2: The Carter III Sessions* — to be "among the best albums of 2007."

Fast-forward to 2008, and it was a year when you couldn't go to any urban music gathering and not hear Wayne's smash singles "Lollipop" or "A Milli" from his sixth studio album *Tha Carter*

Drake and his Young Money/Cash Money Billionaire mentor Lil Wayne
(© Seth Browarnik/startraksphoto.com)

III blaring through speakers. *Blender* magazine named "A Milli" the best rap single of the year, and *Forbes* magazine estimated Lil Wayne's annual earnings at $18 million (U.S.). *Tha Carter III* sold several million copies worldwide.

When Drake was looking to expand his mixtape execution strategy and career, he looked to Wayne, one of his rap heroes. Wayne had appeared as a guest on the blazing last track "Man of the Year" from *Comeback Season*, so from the outside looking in, it appeared the stars were aligning. How did he manage to even get the attention of arguably the world's greatest rapper at this critical juncture in his career? "I met Wayne through a friend of mine,

Cash Money CEO Birdman alongside Drake (© Brad Barket/PictureGroup)

J Prince's son [Jas], who I met on Myspace actually," explained Drake in *Urb*. "We just talked back and forth. He was interested in my music for about a year and a half, ever since the Trey Songz joint, he reached out."

Based in Houston, Jas Prince was the son of one of the most renowned record label executives in hip hop, largely responsible for putting Houston hip hop on the map. Rap-A-Lot Records, which his dad founded, introduced the Geto Boys to a wider hip hop industry dominated by east and west coast talents. Jas was a big champion of Drake in the U.S. and he was connecting him to the high-powered artist and manager formations connected to Weezy and Young Money. Wayne was perpetually inundated with requests from other rappers to collaborate with him, so for Jas to get Wayne to give Drake's music a serious listen was a big deal. "He always pressed Wayne to listen to the music, and one day I guess they had time when they were in Houston he played him about two songs; I think they got through about two and a half songs," said Drake. Clearly impressed by Drake, Wayne reached out directly through Jas's contacts. And where was Drake for this big moment? In a barbershop getting his hair cut. He had called Drake from Jas's phone. When Drake answered, he heard a voice that didn't belong to Jas. It actually sounded like Lil Wayne's. Thinking it was a prank, Drake almost blew the call off. "I didn't wanna believe it so I'm like, 'Whatever, man.' And he's like, 'Yo, this is Weezy,' and I'm [sarcastically] like, 'Yeah, aight.' He's like, 'Yo, this is Weezy, can you get on a plane [to Houston] by tomorrow at 8:00 a.m.?'"

When the number one rapper in the free world makes a request, you do your best to accommodate it, and that's exactly what Drake did. They met in late 2008, at a time Drake was overcoming a break-up. Before he knew it, Drake had spent the next few weeks on Wayne's tour bus traveling through America as part of his I Am Music Tour. "I felt like I hit Houston and got my swag back. I was single, I was with Wayne and it was Houston, I was going nuts, sippin' dank, smoking."

With a potential new management situation on the horizon, the sky now truly felt like it was the limit. Lil Wayne's manager Cortez Bryant remembers clearly the first time he heard and saw Drake's potential and wanted to manage him. "I first heard him when Jas Prince played me a CD [of *Comeback Season*]," he told veteran music industry reporter Larry Leblanc. "I was like, 'Wow. This guy, I can understand everything that he is saying. His music feels so real.' Then when we flew him in, and I met him, it was like, 'Oh, wow. This guy's a star.' His personality just rubbed off. I could tell that he was a genuinely good person."

While Cortez was on the road with Wayne (he DJed for Weezy at the time) and hanging with Drake after the concerts, he came face to face with the popularity of a Canadian TV classic. Cortez didn't really know that Drake was already a big TV star with a pre-existing fanbase — he was just thinking about helping to turn him into a massive hip hop star at the time. "We were in Salt Lake City or Denver, I can't remember what city we were in, but it was in the middle of nowhere in the Midwest. . . . We had a great show. We killed it. There's about 200 people still lined up in front of the stage, most of them women, most of them little white girls screaming. So I'm like, 'I must have done a good job. Wow, they're screaming for me,'" recalled Cortez. "But I start hearing, 'Jimmy, Jimmy.' I'm thinking, 'Who the hell is Jimmy? They are not talking about me.' I look to the right, and I see him waving and smiling. 'Hello, what's going on here?' He whispers over to me, 'I forgot to tell you. I was on this show for, like, seven seasons, called *Degrassi*. Jimmy was my character.' I was like, 'What? You act too? Oh my God.'"

Drake may have been *Degrassi* famous, but he was now operating at a whole new level as a member of the most impressive rap crew in America at the time — Young Money. Young Money Entertainment was an imprint label of Cash Money Records, which was founded by Wayne. Drake's hard work, talent and persistence were starting to pay off, but rolling with America's number one rap crew meant working harder than ever. "You're in the presence of one of the greatest. And I really have to pull my weight, because he's vouching for me, so I better come through," Drake told MuchMusic. While touring, Wayne and Drake were also working on some joint tracks. On their last night together, they recorded three songs. "That just sparked a whole partnership," said Drake. "It was undeniable chemistry — everyone that listened was like, damn, those guys sound good together. We look so different."

And look different together they did. Weezy was a short, multi-tattooed, platinum-jewelry-wearing savant who rhymed off tales of

Drake backstage, following his 2011 BET performance that featured Lil Wayne (not pictured), DJ Khaled and Rick Ross (© Frank Micelotta/PictureGroup)

growing up in the murder capital of the U.S., New Orleans. Drake, on the other hand, was a tall, Jewish, boy-next-door figure who grew up in Toronto's wealthy Forest Hill. Weezy was a veteran of the rap world, whereas Drake was a green former child actor. What was it that made this odd couple click? It's hard to say, though there was some serious mutual admiration happening here. While performing at the MTV Video Music Awards in September 2008, Wayne rapped a verse that wasn't exactly his own, and audience members scratched their heads, wondering if he was performing lyrics from a new song, until he yelled "Drizzy Drake, I love you, bwoy." The lyrics *were* in fact from a Drake verse from a collaborative track Wayne and Birdman had recorded with him called "Money to Blow." It was a huge moment in Drake's career, a metaphorical passing of the rap baton. Overnight, Drake became a well-known entity in hip hop's nerve center, the United States.

Before the mainstream media and major labels really took serious notice of his tremendous game-changing potential, there was another key Wayne-assisted moment in his early career that stood out. On NahRight.com, a highly influential rap blog frequented by music industry tastemakers, Drake's "Ransom" collaboration with Wayne debuted on September 4, 2008. Drake had been raised to an even higher platform. He'd be able to see the rap landscape he would come to conquer, and more importantly, everyone could see him.

65

SO FAR
GONE

Despite all of this hype, Drake was still trying to find his voice, to figure out what made him distinct and stick out from the pack of thousands of emcees and R&B vocalists trying to make it. He didn't want "Replacement Girl," a mushy love song, to define his early career ambitions, because he knew he was a much broader artist than that. And he didn't want to be viewed as an artist who needed to ride Lil Wayne's coattails to get to the top of the *Billboard* charts either.

Touring with Weezy had been more than a marketing tool — he'd been working with some of the best in the business, and on his new mixtape, *So Far Gone*, he wanted to show that he belonged among them. *So Far Gone* was going to be the first time that he would get to work together with his muse 40 on a worthwhile full-length project. Like Drake, 40 was seemingly obsessed with clashing R&B soundscapes with distinctly hip hop ones. He said he adored New York's DJ Clark Kent growing up, because "he would always have the illest R&B remix with a rapper on it. Those were always my favorite joints." Having hung around Drake while he was trying to sculpt this new combo of rap and soul, 40 was in Drake's head already. He had a good sense of what kind of sonic blueprint might perfectly fit the rapper's potent rhyme flows — and it would involve blending the worlds of rap and R&B. Explained 40, "Even as a kid, I've been trying to force-feed R&B to rap music. Make rap more musical."

Rap became a lot more musical when Drake and his old "Replacement Girl" companion Trey Songz wrote and recorded a song called "Successful" with 40 for *So Far Gone.* In the song Drake contemplates his own impending success over a catchy radio-friendly blend of soul crooning supplied by Songz that pretty much sums up the accoutrements of fine rap living (money, cars, women) that they so both desired. The banging 40 backbeat was so good that even hardcore rap enthusiasts could bob their heads to it. The song's video shows a contemplative Drake taking in the Toronto nightlife, prepping for world domination. This fresh sonic blueprint was a harbinger of things to come. Drake and his producer 40 had mastered the R&B-heavy hip hop blend they both loved. "We musically connected first with R&B," 40 told *GQ.* "'Successful' was the most significant turning point where he took one of my beats and worked on it . . . where we discovered that sound, that abstract world we were taking rap music to, between me and him."

The mixtape's first single, "Best I Ever Had," marked the emergence of his other main in-house producer Boi-1da, with whom he had developed great chemistry dating back to some of his biggest early singles, including "Replacement Girl," co-produced with another Toronto area producer T-Minus. "Best I Ever Had" was lauded by *Billboard* as the Hot Rap Song of the Year. Next to the Black Eyed Peas' omnipresent "I Gotta Feeling," it was the only music single that year that urban music fans could hear everywhere; blazing out of Jeeps, malls, community centers, iPod ear buds, speakers at NBA game intermissions — the track was game-changing. In the song Drake raps an ode to an unnamed hottie and provides his views on the lasting impacts of former relationships. The infectious, playful hook could make people simultaneously blush and smile, communicating the complexity of laying out honest feelings about your ex-lovers.

R&B queen Mary J. Blige, who collaborated with Drake on her

"The One" single, commented on this rare songwriting ability, calling him the "savior" of urban music. "The kid Drake is the best," she said. "I love what they're singing about, they're bigging up women again. They're making women feel special. It came to the point where women were just bitches and hoes, and he came around and said, 'You the best.'"

"Best I Ever Had" was the second to last song Drake recorded for the mixtape, and even he was surprised by how well it did. He told MTV News, "When I did it, I was like, 'Cool, it adds a little bounce to [the mixtape],' but I wasn't crazy about it." This song he wasn't crazy about zoomed to number one on the *Billboard* charts. The accolades started pouring in. "Best I Ever Had" and "Successful" both became *Billboard* top 10 hits.

One of the best things about the *So Far Gone* mixtape experience was that Drake was rolling with 40, who was his good friend and jack-of-all-music-trades. For example, when they hit the road on the *So Far Gone* tour, 40 was Drake's production manager, stage manager, stage tech, keyboard tech. Most importantly, 40 was a producer/engineer who could take a song from its rough stages all the way to completion. Parts of *So Far Gone* were recorded while Drake was on tour, and most of it was laid down at 40's condo. Some songs from the mixtape were also mixed and mastered in 40's seventh-floor hotel room at the Beverly Wilshire hotel on a pair of AKG K-240 headphones and an iHome clock radio around Grammy time in early 2009. And a handful of songs including the Peter Bjorn and John–inspired "Let's Call It Off" were actually recorded in a hotel suite. Drake, 40 and company had hung out in and around the hotel for over a week while on tour with Lil Wayne. Lil Wayne had been prepping Drake for this project, giving him tips on his songwriting and rap rhymes to really hit home with listeners this time around. "Wayne told me to just remember it's about your thoughts, you got to think about what you want to say beforehand," Drake told *Rolling Stone*. "And then from there, you make it rhyme or you make it connect. But the more important thing is, what's your message, what's your point."

His past success with "Replacement Girl" was one thing, but by most accounts it was this, his third official mixtape, that really propelled him into the music and pop culture stratosphere. Released for free download on February 13 on his October's Very Own blog, between Thursday, February 12, and Friday, February 13, 2009, over 2,500 comments were left by eager fans seeking news on the impending mixtape slated for release on the following day. By this time Drake had mastered his fresh, new sound, recording equal parts singing and rapping, as a way to separate himself from the hip hop pack. This synthesis would allow him to better convey emotions, and would appeal to a broader fanbase. Sonically, the mixtape represented the perfect blend of hard-hitting hip hop and smoothed out soul grooves and was recorded during a time when, Drake said, "I was into the Roots, Little Brother, Mos Def and other great hip hop music." He was still an unsigned artist at this time, but you couldn't tell by the high quality of the music production, engineered by 40.

Coming in at under 33 minutes, *So Far Gone* included guest spots from rappers like Drake's mentor Lil Wayne and Houston rap legend Bun B, all the way to R&B soulsters du jour Omarion and Lloyd. It was downloaded at a furious pace — 2,000 downloads in the first two hours of release. When almost 40,000 people had downloaded the mixtape in under a week, it became one of the most downloaded mixtapes at that time. While mixtapes are usually released with only moderate fanfare online, this one came with the blogosphere's advance blessings. *Pitchfork* remarked, "*So Far Gone* still scans as one of the most compulsively listenable mixtapes of a great year for mixtapes."

When asked about the meaning of the CD's title, Drake said that the title is intentionally open to multiple interpretations, but that it slyly references how he uses his outsider status to his advantage.

"Toronto is struggling for an icon, but I feel the furthest out there of all my peers," he said. "The only people I feel understand me are the ones close to me. I feel like we live with a very genuine, pure, elevated level. But there's also a distance from others who aren't in my circle. I feel like they don't understand what's going on."

If there was one song that perfectly captured the turbulent nature of working in the music industry, of how adversity can help create good art at times, it was "The Calm." Created when Drake was struggling with his familial relations ("I hated going home . . . I was deep in debt with my family. We were fighting every night.") and living part-time in 40's studio in a downtown Toronto apartment on Fort York Boulevard, it was recorded as a cathartic release for all of the stresses going on in his life. "I remember I had this vicious fight with my uncle on 40's balcony," he told *Fader*. "I had never said such cruel things to anybody; I had never had such cruel things said to me, especially by a family member. 40 could tell I just needed to say something about it. He made me this beat. I wrote the first verse in his bedroom, which is where we used to work. He gave me an opportunity to vent about my serious family situations. That was a definitive moment in my career. That was the first time I had ever said anything like that."

40 recalls that "crazy, crazy moment" as being a major breakthrough in strengthening their musical relationship. He said Drake "showed up with $1,000 worth of champagne and I'm cussing at him because we're all broke and trying to make this shit work! Meanwhile, he's renting Phantoms and shit." But behind the bubbly and the bravado, Drake was just another guy who needed a friend to talk to. "He just came back in the room and said, 'I need to rap. Make me something.' In 45 minutes, I made 'The Calm' and he wrote those bars as I made the beat. Over the next five or six hours, that record unfolded in its entirety."

So Far Gone generated over 30 million plays on Drake's Myspace page, and MTV's Mixtape Daily named it "The Hottest Mixtape of

2009 (So Far)." Not everyone was fully blown away by *So Far Gone*, considering the female-friendly work to be too derivative of Kanye West's *808s & Heartbreak*, but Drake sloughed off these criticisms. "I think any time a rapper sings now, they're going to say that. Just like whenever a rapper uses Auto-Tune, they say that's T-Pain . . . I've been singing way before *808 & Heartbreak*."

With fans far and wide wanting a piece of the wunderkind, Drake took further steps to elevate his legend in his hometown by having NBA superstar LeBron James host his mixtape release party. This was the same James who a few years earlier was ranked at number one in the Forbes Top 20 Earners Under 25, with annual

Friends LeBron James and Drake play off each other's success (© Jesse Grant/WireImage)

earnings of $27 million. Drake had a very easy time cozying up to other young, black, buzzy newsmakers of his generation like LeBron James. The synergy between these two leading newsmakers made so much sense that when James needed a rapper to pen an anthem for the soundtrack to *More Than a Game*, the 2009 documentary about his rise to fame, Drake was handpicked to participate. He kicked off the lead single, "Forever," skilfully rapping the opening verse and soulfully crooning the song's hook. He was in good company on the soundtrack, which featured seasoned rap royalty like Kanye West, Lil Wayne and Eminem.

With *So Far Gone* being rated as the hottest mixtape of 2009, many even began to question the feasibility of releasing music for free, when his brand was already so big, and there was ample opportunity to generate vast sums of revenue from his artistic output. In a *Vibe* magazine interview Drake broke down his smart, brazen rationale to deflect the critics who wondered why he'd still give away his art for free. "Some people are like, 'Why'd you do that for free?'" he said. "If I released that as a retail album, I would've probably been criticized and scrutinized. It wouldn't have gone over as well as the way I did it." Key OVO team member (and Drake's go-to style consultant) Oliver El-Khatib elaborated further: "We've done things very unorthodox and not necessarily in our favor financially, i.e., releasing another piece of work for free. But this is his chance to put out music that's just for the sake of art. He's not answering to anybody. There's no label. This is a position piece — look, I'm an artist."

Drake was confident that his fanbase would fiscally support any new CD he released for commercial consumption, despite being spoiled with all of this free music. And he was right. The underground and online buzz of the *So Far Gone* mixtape got it play on commercial radio, and his team released it about seven months later in a shortened seven-song EP format distributed by Universal. The songs were so popular people were willing to pay for what they could have had for free. The critical acclaim just kept pouring in, as the *Village Voice* referred to the game-changing, genre-blending release as being "an amazing refraction of what rap can be in the decade to come: not rap."

 So Far Gone sold over 500,000 copies, a groundbreaking achievement considering the full-version mixtape was available for free download just over half a year earlier. But *So Far Gone* was always intended to act as a teaser for his first official full-length CD, *Thank Me Later*. Drake hoped that the same frenzied energies his fans exhibited as they downloaded *So Far Gone* for free or bought it in EP form would show up in support of his debut. "You know people have to go buy it and they have to support it or else you're not going to live up to the expectations," he said. "But hopefully we can channel that same energy into this project."

SMART-PHONE SCRIB-ING AND RHYMING

It could be argued that rap music, as an offshoot of hip hop culture, emerged from West African griot traditions and then was later pioneered by African-American spoken-wordsmiths of the '70s led by the late Gil Scott-Heron and the Last Poets. In modern day rap lore, rooted in late '70s New York street culture, there are a few significant stories that link early wordsmiths who might've freestyle rhymed, oftentimes not writing down their verses. When rap music's first hit single "Rapper's Delight" — arguably its most famous historical single — was released in 1979, the song allegedly contained verses that Sugar Hill Gang group member Big Bank Hank lifted from respected underground rapper Grandmaster Caz's written rhyme books. While Caz is reported to have not received any royalties for his songwriting contribution to the track, the importance of the rap rhyme book shows up early in rap's history.

Rhyme books have always played a crucial role in how rappers record their thoughts and rhymes, and then translate them into full-blown songs. On a *60 Minutes* broadcast in 2011, Eminem went to great lengths explaining his songwriting process and the importance of his collection of books of handwritten lyrics. Others, like old-school rap legend Rakim, one of the best rap songwriters of all time, once began writing his rhymes in wild graffiti lettering out of fear that people would mimic his writing style — a fear created when he once lost his rhyme notepad. Rakim links writing down lyrics with "consciousness in hip hop." He explained, "If you sit down, it means you're going to put in time. It's really important for the culture, and it definitely shows substance."

But that was then, and this is now. With the advent of smartphones, the rap notepad seems to have gone the way of vinyl — a niche method only employed by purists. By most accounts Drake is the millennial generation rapper who helped usher in and then popularize the rise of the smartphone-aided rapper. Instead of whipping out classic rhyme books to record their tracks in a studio or compile rhymes while in transit, many rappers of today rely on their smartphones to record their works-in-progress, which then become lyrics to songs. For Drake, the smartphone became mightier than the pen, especially as he became a professional emcee. "All Drake's raps for eternity have been written inside of a BlackBerry," revealed 40, of the new rap penmanship popularized by his friend. "I mean to the point where if he doesn't have a BlackBerry, we gotta go get somebody who's got one. I've had dummy BlackBerrys around, that I just pull out for him to write on if he needs one, that don't actually even work." Even Drake admitted, "I can't write my raps on paper . . . the BlackBerry keys — my thumbs were made for touching them."

Drake's BlackBerry rap legend really began when he was out on the road riding high off the *So Far Gone* buzz. On March 16, 2009, the internet lit up with "live" clips of Drake freestyle rapping from his BlackBerry on the highly rated Hot 97 FM *Funkmaster Flex* show. In this widely viewed clip, Drake furiously spits out his rhymes after he carefully scrolls his BlackBerry. It was from this day forward that Drake became known as the smartphone rap guy, and some comedic spoofs appeared immediately thereafter on YouTube. (Comedian Affion Crockett's is gut busting.) Drake explained that it wasn't even his intention to rap verses read off his smartphone — he simply wasn't quite prepared in advance for the potential request from Funkmaster Flex to perform a "live" rap on air. "It was such a rookie hip hop moment. . . . I just wasn't prepared," he said. Acknowledging a slight shift in how his generation might view a freestyle rhyme, he still has a tremendous respect for the writing processes that came before him: "I appreciate the elements of hip hop. I appreciate a guy like Common who goes city to city and just spits at the crowd for 10 minutes about everything he sees. I admire talent like that, because that's just not my creative process."

Drake is credited by many for popularizing this new digitized rap rhyme book tradition. (Years later when Drake performed at a BlackBerry Torch launch party in August 2010 in Los Angeles, it was like his narrative had come full circle.) Drake has further established himself as a wordsmith who is invested in fully utilizing other digital tools to their fullest potential. Drake and his team launched a full-on assault on the world wide web when he began tweeting on March 28, 2009, at @Drakkardnoir (he now tweets at @Drake), as a way to keep his legions of followers tapped into his daily musings, all the while continuing to releasing free downloadable music and communicate routinely through his October's Very Own blog. While Drake only began blogging in July 2009, and tweeting a few months before that, he was now perpetually trending, riding the wave of his popularity, which showed no signs of breaking.

RACE
RELATIONS

In the rap world, is it even at all possible to be both simultaneously 'hood and Hasidic? There's much debate over whether Drake can be considered the kosher king of contemporary rap music. Where exactly does Drake rank in the pantheon of Jewish rappers? Is he the Best Jewish Rapper alive? Or quite simply the Best Black Jewish Rapper ever? The reality is that he doesn't have that much competition. In the history of hip hop, an accomplished, long-running solo emcee who is Jewish, or publically claims his or her Jewishness, is a rare thing. Outside of the multi-million-selling Beastie Boys (Mike Diamond, Adam Horovitz and the late Adam Yauch), weed-smoking frat boy rapper Asher Roth ("I Love College"), whose father was Jewish, and other more obscure underground hip hop acts like horrorcore emcee Necro, or MC Serch of 3rd Bass, who experienced more mainstream fame for their diss of Vanilla Ice than for their catalog of music, Israeli-American Yoni "Sneakas" Ben-Yehuda, who recorded a brilliant take on Big L's classic "Ebonics" ("Hebonics 101"), or New York's Hoodie Allen ("Bagels and Beats"), but outside of this short list few rappers publicly claiming Judaism have made much impact on Billboard charts or impacted a wide swath of secular youth across cultures.

In hip hop, many of the more high-profile Jews tended to work in the background of the industry, and there have been quite a number who've played pivotal roles as executives, going back to rap's genesis. There's Tom Silverman, who founded the seminal Tommy Boy Records (responsible for iconic acts like Naughty by Nature and House of Pain); Def Jam's co-founder Rick Rubin, who worked with his business partner-in-crime Russell Simmons to cross rap music over to pop charts with Run-DMC and the Beastie Boys; Steve Rifkind, who signed the Wu-Tang Clan; and Warner Music executive Lyor Cohen, who was responsible for helping to fund the controversial Murder Inc. Records with Ja Rule.

When you look for rappers who are both African-American and Jewish, the list of influential figures gets even shorter. The short history of black Jewish rappers contains some bizarre stories, beginning with one of Drake's labelmates at Cash Money Records, Shyne. Shyne, whose father is the prime minister of Belize, was implicated in a 1999 New York City club shooting that left three people injured and the reputations of P. Diddy and Jennifer Lopez, his two accomplices, slightly scarred. Shyne served nine years of a 10-year sentence in various NYC correctional facilities. While in jail, he became a strict Orthodox Jew, and upon his release in 2009 he moved to Jerusalem to practice his faith with more commitment. He also changed his name to Moshe Levi Ben-David to align more closely to his grandmother's Jewish heritage. He has collaborated with fellow Jewish urban music artist Matisyahu, and as recently as June 2011 Shyne was releasing new music to honor the first solar field in Israel. Other more obscure black Jewish rappers like Flatbush-based Yitzchak "Y-Love" Jordan, like Drake, have also struggled to straddle the secular and racial fence. As arguably New York's only visible black ultra-Orthodox Jewish rapper, the Baltimore bred emcee who relocated to Brooklyn and converted to Judaism in his early 20s said that the way he is viewed by his own Jewish community is troubling. "Being black affects everything," he told the *New York Daily News*. "I had kids stare at me like I was a gremlin in Borough Park."

Many successful musicians in popular culture tend not to promote themselves within a religious framework, to avoid any discussion of things unrelated to their art. Drake is an anomaly because he actively promotes his Jewish faith. Despite Jewish talk show host Jimmy Kimmel once suggesting that Drake could harm his career by publicly embracing his Jewish and Canadian identity, Drake seemed to emphasize these traits that separate him from the pack. On the cover of *Vibe*'s December 2009 issue, under the heading "Is Drake Hip Hop's New Religion?" Drake is seen sporting a diamond-studded Chai (a Hebrew symbol representing "life") chain. In other very public arenas, like at the 2010 Juno Awards, he made it a priority to shout out his "very Jewish mother." While many of today's Jewish pop superstars never really actively participate in a greater national Jewish discourse, Drake's public embrace of his religious identity makes him unique. Though he doesn't have to discuss his faith much if he doesn't want to, Drake tends to embrace interview opportunities with Jewish culture magazines like *Heeb*, enlightening fans and readers alike on items like his long-held desire to travel to Israel and his mother's hope that he'll marry "a nice Jewish girl."

Drake's so proud of his heritage that to honor Passover, he

decided he would "get re–bar mitzvah'd as a recommitment to the Jewish religion" with friends Trey Songz, Birdman, DJ Khaled and Weezy in his half serious video shoot for "HYFR (Hell Ya Fuckin' Right)." The video even features archival footage of seven-year-old Drake at his cousin's bar mitzvah. While some might question the appropriateness of featuring sexually explicit lyrics and profanity that appear in the clip alongside footage of a serious rite of passage in a religious house of worship, the video's director, X, insisted they were respectful: "We made sure it was all legitimate. We didn't make any jokes. We took little liberties with the afterparty. That's more of a 'What if' situation. . . . if you're watching, you see Drake's Torah and the reading of the lines. It's like these two worlds coming together. There's nothing in there that's disrespectful. We had a rabbi from the temple right there the whole time." Drake's bar mitzvah, which was held at an Italian restaurant, was much more modest than his wild music video version, but Drake has fond memories of his real-life ceremony, notably slow dancing to the Backstreet Boys' "I Want It That Way" with a girl named Heidi Gold. "It was the song of the night," he said.

Drake's pride in his background even caused some controversy when he wondered to TMZ if he or TMZ creator Harvey Levin was the better Jew. Said Drake, "I don't know. I'm one of the best Jews to ever do it. Ever in life." A week after Drake's TMZ outburst hit the blogosphere, Jewish rap/reggae musician Matisyahu reacted to Drake's declaration with some cutting criticisms. "Drake is a pretty good man. He's got his thing, but it's different than what I do," said Matisyahu, who's jokingly called a "Jewmaican" because of his propensity to sing with a Jamaican "nation language" flow inspired by the reggae music he adopted. "He's Jewish, but he's not representing Judaism. He happens to be Jewish just like Bob Dylan happened to be Jewish, but what I'm doing is really tapping into my roots and culture, and trying to blend that with the mainstream . . . Drake's being Jewish is just a by-product."

From that point onwards, a mild "kosher beef" between the two had developed online, with some wondering who was a genuine or faux Jew performer, and the best Jewish rapper around. When 20-year-old Pittsburgh-based Jewish rapper Mac Miller, a Wiz Khalifa protégé, entered the fray and took some comedic shots at Drake saying that he was "the coolest Jewish rapper," the debate got more silly than serious. On Twitter he later half-jokingly suggested to Drake that maybe they could both collaborate on a Hanukah song. Responding on Twitter, Drake said, "Haaaaaa . . . shit like this can only be settled in Tel Aviv. Birthright sound clash."

Certainly living in a world where both religion and race *really do* matter, Drake's embrace of the N-word in his rhyme repertoire has created some interesting discussion on how far North America has come in its treatment of race issues

Scooping into a giant birthday cake, Drake celebrates his 25th in Vegas (© Santiago Interiano/PR Photos)

especially within hip hop culture circles, where the term is widely employed. Drake grew up adoring the racially conflicted Michael Jackson. As a child Drake watched and studied MJ's *Moonwalker* religiously, learned every dance move from it, and he pays lyrical homage to his influence on "Over," with an N-word twist.

When his musical hero Michael Jackson said it didn't matter if we were black or white, he clearly wasn't referring to using the N-word in hip hop. Because it does. Whether the word itself should be used by anyone is in itself a divisive issue, the race of the people using it is just as controversial. When actor Gwyneth Paltrow tweeted an image of herself, The-Dream, Ty Ty and Bee High at a Kanye West and Jay-Z concert on June 1, 2012, with the caption "Ni✳✳as in paris for real," she was lambasted in the blogosphere despite simply repeating the actual name of the Jay-Z and Kanye West song (and she even used maledicta symbols in her tweet). Others, like white rapper V-Nasty, a member of the White Girl Mob, headed up by Kreayshawn, was also taken to task by both black (Game) and white (Machine Gun Kelly, Yelawolf) rappers for carelessly using the N-word in her raps in 2011, reigniting debates around the polarizing word. Respected rapper Common — who uses the N-word in his own rhymes — struggled when hearing Caucasian cast members uttering those words while filming the *Hell on Wheels* TV series, despite the fact they were only acting. "Even if you try to think that they're acting, it still just doesn't feel right," he told *NY Mag.* "You get that feeling like, 'Man, this is not good.'" Rap cognoscenti Chuck D of Public Enemy tweeted his concerns over the current frequency in the usage of the word, and wondered aloud about who exactly is uttering it so much. "I swear I ain't never seen the N-word as much as I do HERE on the damn web," he tweeted on May 6, 2012, from his @mrchuckd account. "I would just love to see these faces behind the typing of this word."

As a Jewish-identifying half-white rapper, with some of his closest family members (mother Sandi), best friends (producer Noah "40" Shebib) and business associates (creative director Oliver El-Khatib) being non-black, does Drake make them feel squeamish when he routinely utters the N-word in his music? Do they sing along to his many N-word utterances in "Nigga Like Me" without cringing, or do they leave it alone? Or are both sides of his black and white identity and his relationships unmoved by all things N? As someone whose Jewish side might be more sensitive to issues around race, should Drake be thinking through his casual employment of the N-word in his rhymes? It's an important question, in a world where race does matter, and where Facebook groups like "Drake is NOT dark enough to be aloud [sic] to say the N-word" or "If u see DRAKE using the N-Word, punch 'em [sic] in the face!" exist. Drake has publicly weighed in on using the loaded pejorative term. "I personally do use it in my music, it's a tough thing because I never feel when I'm doing it that I'm wrong," he admitted to *Notable Interviews* in 2007, way before the million-dollar recording contracts and *Billboard* chart dominance. "Just because I say that word, I'm never necessarily surrounding it by other phrases that are bringing down black people; if anything, I think my music shows that black men can be intelligent, that black men can have real thoughts as opposed to just shooting guns and doing all this stupid stuff that maybe society thinks that we do as rappers, as black men." He added, "At the end of the day it's a racial slur, it's something that hasn't clicked with me yet, maybe I'm too young, or maybe I haven't delved that deep into the black culture to be like, 'I'm never gonna say that again.'"

Almost five years later in a March 2012 interview with Tim Westwood, he mused on how the word, while still offensive, has become so deeply ingrained in hip hop that it's hard to look back: "I definitely don't want to be the guy who promotes the use of the word. I don't think there's anybody that necessarily deserves to use it, we've all established that its not the greatest word in the world. But you know at the same time it's a word that a lot of us just grew up with in our vocabulary.... I'm 25 years old and I'll be honest with you, no matter who you are, its just part of our culture unfortunately."

TRIPLE THREAT:

Rapper, Singer, Actor

Drake's reputation as one of the best rappers in the biz is too limiting a definition, as he seemingly attracted audiences outside of the hip hop box. R&B lovers also loved his sound. And he had developed a large following for his acting career, compliments of *Degrassi*. He was now a rare, hybridized super talent.

Drake sings. But he also raps. Sound simple? It's not really. "The balance of singing and rapping has been blurred ever since I did *So Far Gone*," he explained. Many of his monster singles typically see him both sing and rap, something many burgeoning Toronto urban music talents had grown up witnessing with combo rapper/singer k-os tinkering with this sonic template. "I like to incorporate singing into my verses," he said. "And then I feel like it allows people a break from just constant rapping, rapping, rapping, you know? I think it's great to incorporate melodies into the songs that I write."

To date, no one has ever really heard Drake exercise his vocal chops as a straight R&B vocalist over a full-length CD sans hip hop, partly because he pulled the plug on his much talked about R&B mixtape tentatively titled *It's Never Enough.* What we do know is that in the history of hip hop there have been few rappers who, like Lauryn Hill, have been able to pull off the rare feat of being respected as much for their rap skills — lyrical delivery, flow and rhyme skills — as they are for their ability to blow, much like a great soul singer would. In recent urban music history, there are a fair number of rap talents whose attempts at singing are mediocre at best, from Kanye West and Pharrell Williams to Wyclef Jean and Biz Markie way before them. Still other performers like St. Louis's Nelly or Long Beach's Domino toed the line between rapper and singer, defying easy categorization.

When you throw acting into the mix, Queen Latifah has arguably come the closest to perfecting this trifecta. While Queen Latifah is more widely known in the rap community as a proto-feminist emcee recording seminal songs like "Ladies First," she has also released critically acclaimed full-length jazz albums (*The Dana Owens Album, Trav'lin' Light*) that showcase her wide-ranging vocal talents. She has also racked up a long list of TV and film credits, including providing her voice alongside Drake in the fourth instalment of *Ice Age.*

While it takes considerable talent to practice these disparate crafts, certainly the rap-croon effects heard prominently in Drake's music might also be viewed as a by-product of the iPod Generation. Many millennial musicians grew up listening to music according to the shuffle function on their iPods, which made genre-hopping the norm, not the exception. This abandonment of music segregation can be seen in modern commercial rap as it continues to drift further away from hip hop's basic elements toward a new, hybrid sound that blends rap, R&B, electronic and even alt-rock (witness the success of B.o.B, Kid Cudi or Death Grips). And while no one's anointing Drake the new Sam Cooke or Curtis Mayfield just yet, there's no question that this half-singing, half-rapping Toronto native is helping change the face of rap firsthand by being a mirror to modern-day genre-blending music realities.

There was a time in hip hop when the whole notion of R&B singers, male or female, appearing on hardcore hip hop tracks was considered sacrilege, a formula that would eventually water down the genuine hip hop product. Now 16 years later T-Pain (who popularized Auto-Tune) has any hip hopper waving a microphone believing they can sing.

It was deemed an honorable thing to do when Kanye West recorded his *808s & Heartbreak* CD, singing for the majority of the release as a vocal tribute to his mother Donda West, who had just passed away from a complication of her plastic surgery. *808s & Heartbreak* is a must-listen for Drake enthusiasts, only because its sonic template is largely thought to have influenced Drake's sound from *So Far Gone* to today. In a *Vibe* magazine interview Drake slyly distanced himself from the subconscious Kanye influences that showed up in his music. He told them he thought the comparison was "just about a rapper singing," and added, "It's about being genuine and really striking a chord with women. To be honest I don't think there's many songs on *808s & Heartbreak* that really do that."

The decision for Drake to sing on his own tracks isn't just Drake flexing his vocal muscles. For example, why would Drake wait for studio time and pay a guest singer when he can do it himself, and well? Rappers like Ja Rule popularized this strategy and figured out that the best way to capture people is with an easy and repeatable melody that could bring in female R&B listeners. It has been long

Drake with BET's Debra L. Lee and Beyoncé, a superstar who's surpassed triple-threat status (© Adrian Sidney/PictureGroup)

thought that female fans will more easily gravitate to hip hoppers with soulful sensibilities, the melodies taking an edge off some of the harsh content in their verses. Drake commented on how the seemingly disparate worlds of hip hop and R&B were becoming more interchangeable, and how R&B singers were also appropriating what was originally considered rap swag or attitude to their seemingly softer songs. "This generation is all about partying and living life. The soundtrack to that lifestyle is not a Case or Joe record. Dudes will tell me they're not even into R&B like that, but they appreciate my swag on it." Drake also considered his R&B songwriting strategy more closely aligned with how a rapper like Jay-Z might compose verses, further eroding the distinctions between rappers and crooners. "The way Jay and Wayne write rap, I write R&B," admitted Drake. "I don't write lyrics down on paper. . . . The other day, I was in the studio with Alicia Keys, and I wrote two songs just speaking to her. I wish I could write that way for rap."

Drake's chart dominance as a songwriter able to pen catchy R&B hooks is particularly noteworthy, a skill few rappers can claim. On "Money to Blow," he actually refers to himself as "Captain Hook." And justifiably so. One standalone feature in many of Drake's hit songs is his ability to craft catchy melodies that are quite easy to memorize and recite after a few listens. But it wasn't always this way. In a MTV segment on Drake, his assistant and good friend Courtnee, a.k.a. Queen Shmink, said that Drake had been toying around with this melodious R&B-meets-rap formula many years before his official recording success. She claimed that Drake recorded a song titled "Single Again" that is thought to be the first rap-meets-R&B hybrid song that he ever made. Apparently he played it for close friends and family, and lacking confidence, tried to play the song off as not being his own. In fact, the first time he played it for Courtnee, he reportedly pretended the song was recorded by his friend, asking her, "What did you think of my friend?" But when his mom walked in the room and said, "Aubrey

— oh, you're playing the song where you rap and you sing," the jig was up. Courtnee's initial response to the song? "He raps and sings in it, and it's so bad." *Comeback Season's* "Brand New," the first widely available song Drake sings on without rapping, got a better reaction. After being released into the internet ether, it took on a life of its own: Wayne remixed it, and YouTube is filled with fans performing their own renditions.

Drake continues to pursue his passion for R&B, though when he sings, he relies on Auto-Tune on occasion. Though the emcee has natural singing talent, his vocal coach Dionne Osbourne (from legendary vocal trainer Jan Smith's team) once remarked that he feels the need to take formal vocal training to grow his art — Auto-Tune aids or not. "You know what I like about Drake is he really wants to get better," she said. "When he performs he's getting better and better performances. And other people notice this, it's not just fine-tuning stuff... honestly, he had the tools, he just didn't know what he was doing with them."

Certainly, when Stevie Wonder's daughter revealed her dad had used Drake's "Brand New" to warm up for his shows, it was clear Drake's brand of R&B (that's Rap & Blues) was resonating with some serious soul initiators. Stevie Wonder has since become a friend of Drake, appearing at his annual OVO festival in Toronto in 2011 as a special guest, where he performed six songs, and playing harmonica on *Take Care's* "Doing It Wrong."

DRAKE BREAKS IN AMERICA

Texas rap legend Bun B (UGK) joins Drake onstage at Toronto's Sound Academy (© ShotByDrew)

By the summer of 2008, there was no disputing that Lil Wayne was

the most respected rapper in the hip hop universe. As Wayne's repu-

tation grew to mammoth proportions, so too did Drake's because of

their friendship and artistic affiliation. Rarely a day went by without

a Drake and/or Weezy rumor or sighting online. On the Toronto stop

of his I Am Music tour at Toronto's Air Canada Centre in January

2009, Wayne brought out his protégé on the mic to sing and spit

some verses on "Ms. Officer" and "Pop Bottles," much to the surprise

and delight of the audience. There could be no greater endorsement

to the 20,000-strong crowd. "To be completely honest with you, I was nervous," he told *Peace!* magazine of his hometown coronation. "Not about forgetting my lyrics, or tripping, or anything like that. But up until that moment I could never be sure if I had any fans in my own city — 20,000 people is a lot of people to win over, and even if one-quarter don't like me that's still intimidating. But it ended up being a great night."

Having now secured his hometown's full attention, as well as southern U.S. rap audiences because of his Wayne affiliation, he now had to focus his efforts on New York. Despite the New York hip hop scene's recent sagging rap fortunes — next to Jay-Z or ASAP Rocky, most of today's rap heroes like 2 Chainz can be found in the south — it's still considered rap's epicenter, the city where the art form was birthed and popularized. Being successful here means you've truly made it.

With all signs pointing to Drake as rap's next big superstar, Drake was invited to perform at Hot 97 FM's Who's Got Next showcase at S.O.B.'s, a legendary New York City club, in May 2009. This was his unofficial debut, as over 300 tastemakers, influencers and music industry mavens including Talib Kweli, Ryan Leslie, Lyor Cohen and Kanye West would be in attendance. Drake lived up to the hype and performed a blazing set of songs set to instrumentals played by his official tour DJ and friend Future the Prince, a Toronto-based East African DJ whose star rose as a club DJ due to his deft video-mixing skills. In 2007 he became Drake's DJ and later showed his stuff at some of North America's largest events, from Grammy and MTV Award events, to Super Bowl and NBA All-Star game events. At one point in the show Drake was joined onstage by southern underground rap legend Bun B, whom he had befriended earlier on in his career, and that went a long way to solidifying his street cred.

With this one show, Drake had conquered New York City. As *Billboard*'s report from the S.O.B.'s show put it, "Drake . . . has the biggest buzz in hip hop right now." Everybody wanted to jump on the

Drake bandwagon now, and a whirlwind of promotional activity happened to secure his position. By June 7 his unscheduled cameo at Hot 97 FM's Summer Jam concert at Giants Stadium, a key annual event for New York's rap scenesters, was wholly approved. A week later Kanye West, who was becoming more interested in directing videos, agreed to direct "Best I Ever Had." The video was shot at Brooklyn's Bishop Ford Central Catholic High School, and Jay-Z and Common were spotted on set. The same day, Drake appeared on *The Tonight Show* with Conan O' Brien alongside Jamie Foxx, performing his guest verse from Foxx's hit "Digital Girl" single. "Best I Ever Had" became hip hop's summer anthem, zooming to number one on *Billboard* charts. It was Drake's world, and everyone was just living in it.

EMI west coast creative president/head of urban "Big" Jon Platt, who had developed quite the reputation for scooping up marquee talents like Jay-Z, Kanye West, Usher and Beyoncé ahead of the curve, had been tracking Drake's movements from the jump, relying on his instincts as a former Denver-based DJ. "Drake is the whole package: music, lyrics, flow; everything," said Platt. "His *So Far Gone* mixtape is better to me than a lot of people's albums because it's all original, new songs." After having spent weeks studying the Drake phenomenon, Platt flew to Canada and spent about five hours with him. "I went to see him in Toronto well before everything really exploded," Platt told *Billboard* about snatching Drake before anyone else did. "We just hung out all day and had a great conversation. I knew then that he was the real deal." A seasoned industry veteran, Platt was amazed at his skill set, maturity and composure. "I didn't think they were making stars like Drake anymore. But I knew right then the kid had it, that special thing." By the time the BET Awards took place in Los Angeles on June 28, 2009, Platt had allegedly signed Drake to a publishing deal — in the artist's dressing room.

While this summer of 2009 was hot on all fronts for Drake,

he had to be more careful than ever with the artistic decisions he was going to make. Drake got some bad press after the 2009 BET Awards, following a Young Money crew and Lil Wayne perfor-mance of sexually charged songs like "Every Girl" and "Best I Ever Had" that featured a group of young girls — Wayne's nine-year-old daughter and her friends — dancing onstage. Drake humbly and immediately issued a sincere apology and admitted that the perfor-mance was done in poor taste.

Drake had another fire to extinguish after the release of his "Best I Ever Had" video, which features Drake playing coach to a female basketball squad. The video features so many close-ups of women's breasts that it was jokingly dubbed "Breast I Ever Had." Was it director Kanye West's vision to reduce these women to body parts (the video's breast focus closely resembles West's "The New Workout Plan" video that had been released six years prior)? No one's sure. But rather than play the blame game, Drake wisely used the mixed reviews of his video as a teachable moment, later apologizing. "I guess one thing I didn't consider is what the song personally means to a lot of women," Drake told MTV News. "To those women, I apologize. I do apologize. My intention wasn't to put anyone down. It was to make them laugh. I wanted people to see something visually different."

While all of this was going on, Drake was engaged in a seven-digit bidding war, brokered by Cash Money, to secure his signature on a recording contract. He'd achieved huge success on his own, but he needed the industry onside to take things to the next level. In the end, he signed directly to Aspire, a company co-run by his manager (and Young Money exec) Cortez Bryant, with major label distribution through Universal Republic. Universal Motown Republic Group won the Drake stakes, signing him for a rumored advance of around $2 million, in a deal that allowed him to keep his publishing rights. Drake told ABC News, "I wanted to own a lot of my future endeavors and my past catalog because I feel like we did do this ourselves." The deal broke down as a joint venture between Young Money and Cash Money, with Universal Republic distributing his music. In this deal, Drake reportedly gave up 25 percent of his music sales earnings as a distribution payment to the label.

Drake's management were unbending in their belief that he should be viewed as an independent artist, so hardcore fans wouldn't think he was selling out. The deal allowed him the benefits of big label distribution and promotion but left his management structure and artistic control untouched. "Today is definitely a comfortable day for me, having my team now that's been in place for a couple of years," Drake said upon signing his groundbreaking deal. "It's something new, but it feels familiar." Drake was openly excited about having a corporate structure around him to help push his independent music movement. "Independent is a funny term," he once remarked. "I can go independent, but you need distribution, period. You need somebody to distribute your record and you need that army that a label has to really push the record."

The expectation surrounding Drake's debut full-length had grown so much that pundits wondered how he'd be able to live up to the hype or match the brilliance of *So Far Gone*. Drake said he was going to call his major label debut *Thank Me Later*. "Greatness takes time," he explained to ABC News about the meaning of the CD title. "That's why my upcoming album is called *Thank Me Later*, because I know for a fact how much pressure is riding on it, and I know that right away there's gonna be people just waiting [to say], 'No, that's not it, he's not the one.'" The CD was originally scheduled for an early spring 2009 release but took longer than expected, given the importance of his official debut. "This is my first album and it takes a lot for me to commit to a song and be like, 'I like this enough that I'm gonna put it on the album,'" he said. "It's gotta be something that I feel is timeless and is better than anything that I've ever done."

To keep his fans and the media at bay while they awaited his official offering, Drake stayed in the public eye, doing live guest spots on TV and performing in a series of concerts. For him the most exciting appearance was as a guest at Jay-Z's concert on Halloween in Toronto, when Jay-Z invited Drake onstage to perform his hit "Successful." "I'll never forget that," he told *Paper* magazine. "I must have looked in the eyes of 40 people I know in the first 20 rows. There were ex-girlfriends, guys who hated me, people who loved me, my mother — and it was just like, 'This is it.'" Drake declared that this Jay-Z moment was the time when he felt truly validated by the hip hopperati: no one in Toronto, a city of small rap dreams, could think it was possible for a home-grown rapper to be rolling with the big American dogs. "There was a big rumor around the city: is Drake close enough to Jay where he would bring me out? And people were like, 'No, it would never happen,'" he said. To the casual observer, Drake's Jay-Z moment should not have come as a complete surprise. Toronto's Very Own Drake had played a packed

Sound Academy concert a number of months before that in May 2009, and had over 2,000 people in attendance, most of whom sang and rapped along word-for-word to his hits — and this was *before* he had a major label backing him.

Another strategy from his camp to keep his name on the lips of the growing rap nation eager to learn more about *Thank Me Later* was to leak info about some of his collaborations, ones that he knew would pique the interest of the media. He had already been featured on the Timbaland-produced first single from Jay-Z's *The Blueprint 3*, "Off That," though he had only performed on the hook. On December 2009, Drake revealed that his long-anticipated collaboration with Jay-Z for *Thank Me Later*, a song titled "Light Up" (co-produced by Toronto production trio Tone Mason) was done. "Everybody is looking for this one joint with me and Jay, so that needs to happen," he had remarked a few months earlier. "My goal at this point is to keep making that organic music. I don't wanna feel pressure now that I have a single and music that's hot." Drake's Jay-Z envy had already been well documented in his song "Fear," where he essentially argues in one verse that Jay-Z could be his generation's Notorious B.I.G. or Tupac.

2009 was turning into the Year of the Drake. He capped off the year in December 2009 by receiving a pair of Grammy nominations based on the strength of his mixtape songs. Whether you were a rap fan or not, his Grammy feat was unprecedented, and just added to his growing music industry lore. "I can honestly say that there was a period in my life where I was in high school and I used to have trouble going to sleep at an early hour because I used to sit there and dream about hearing my name called at a Grammy nomination press conference," he said. Not only was he nominated for the music industry's most prestigious honor but he was asked to close out the 2010 Grammy Awards in January performing on the "Forever" posse cut alongside rap icons Lil Wayne and Eminem, with blink-182's Travis Barker on drums.

Leading up to the performance he was both nervous and contemplative. "I had rehearsals today with Eminem, and he was just like, 'Look, man, if you ever get nervous, just look at me, look me in my eyes, and I'm gonna give you that reassurance, 'cause I know you're gonna kill it, don't ever doubt yourself.'" Standing tall alongside these rap icons, performing a track he contributed to for his good friend LeBron James's *More Than a Game* soundtrack, he launched into his verse and killed it. While he didn't take home any awards that night, at the very least Drake had proven he had the goods to be red-carpet material.

THANK
HIM
LATER

There was no disputing that Drake was living as close to a charmed life as anyone could. He was now genuinely independently wealthy, hanging with the big dogs like LeBron and he could pick and choose his next career moves. Though as his popularity was soaring to dizzying heights, he was not immune to the usual distractions and controversies that affect world-class entertainers.

Drake had already endured his fair share of adversity when he was on the come-up in Toronto. There's a part of hip hop culture's ethos where, almost as a rite of passage, rappers will duel on the mic and sometimes off of it. And Drake was now competition. Certainly, the narrative that painted him as the preppy, middle-class, half-white kid from Forest Hill who's had a fairly easy life and even easier time ascending to the top of the rap game seemed to make him an easier target in a hip hop culture where 'hood authenticity still counts for something, despite the fact that many of the culture's rap heroes, from Eminem and Rick Ross to T.I. and Jay-Z, transcended their 'hood origins to become millionaires many times over.

Back in 2009 when Drake admitted in a *New York Times* feature, "I feel unsafe in Toronto at all times," most people outside "Toronto the Good" would think he was exaggerating. Despite its reputation as being one of the best cities to live in in the world, there are numerous low-income Toronto 'hoods (dubbed "Priority Neighborhoods"), where a disproportionate number of racialized youth reside who suffer from government neglect. In these 'hoods, blocks do get hot with gun violence sadly ravaging communities from Scarborough to Jane-Finch, Rexdale to Regent Park. On July 17, 2012, Drake tweeted that the "senseless violence in Toronto has to stop" in the wake of a mass shooting at a Scarborough block party. And few outside of these communities seem to care enough to intervene.

After having played a wealthy kid and basketball star who gets shot and ends up in a wheelchair, Drake's real life success and money might have unfairly made him a target, so he had to be careful he didn't get shot and end up in a wheelchair for real. One day that fear was nearly realized. His troubles began on May 31, 2009, in Toronto's Little Italy neighborhood, when he "wasn't even really Drake yet" he told *GQ*. Drake was allegedly robbed at double gunpoint while out on a date. Just back from tour, Drake said, "I knew it was a setup, because I had on a sweater and a jacket. But when they banged on the car window with a gun and opened the door, the first thing he said was 'Yo, run that chain.' They didn't rob [my date], and her purse was sitting right there. So I was like, 'OK, yup — you set the whole thing up.'" Drake was robbed of $4,000 U.S. in cash and some jewelry.

In a rap universe where "no snitching" codes are the highest law, fellow Toronto rapper Big Page accused Drake of reporting the crime to police, arguably accelerating the dislike some Toronto-area rappers had for him. Page, who had recorded the stellar Juno-nominated "I'm Still Fly" song with Drake, tweeted, "How u gonna rep Toronto on a big scale and be a snitch at the same time???" In an interview with the *Globe and Mail*, Big Page elaborated on his disappointment: "When he was robbed, he was with goons — friends who represented a certain lifestyle. You're supposed to follow the code of that lifestyle, the code of the street and keep your mouth shut." Drake stayed relatively silent on the issue, not revealing whether he did in fact file a police report, but the most lasting consequence of the public beef may have been Drake developing a thicker skin when dealing with his music industry peers.

That thick skin could sometimes also mean staying silent when fellow artists expressed their dislike of his music. For example, Guinness record–holding avant indie rock pianist Chilly Gonzales, a fellow Jewish-Canadian performer who has dabbled in rap himself, was frank about his lack of admiration for the urban music star. When asked about Drake's *So Far Gone* sampling of his composition "The Tourist," he told Canadian fashion magazine *Corduroy*, "I must confess, I'm not a Drake fan. I guess Canadians should be proud that they finally have the closest thing they'll ever have to a credible hip hop personality, but I'm sorry, I'm just not a fan." It's not clear whether this slight got back to Drake, but by the time they shared the stage at the 2011 Juno Awards — performing a cover of "Informer" by Toronto reggae artist Snow together — everything appeared to be kosher between the two.

With *Thank Me Later* the stakes got much higher, unleashing a slew of new distractions that couldn't so easily be ignored. He had to deal with unauthorized versions of his music being released (*The*

Girls Love Drake), Playboy Records suing his camp for unauthorized use of samples on "Best I Ever Had," claims that he had a rapping little brother Tory Lanez and even promoters booking fake Drake concerts in places like Pennsylvania or South Africa without his permission. The only things missing in the Drake media circus were claims from women of birthing a love child and a reality TV show.

As Drake's star rose, many wondered what was happening with his relationship with Lil Wayne. People suggested that Drake's buzz was almost surpassing that of his mentor, and some were even saying that Drake was Wayne's secret ghostwriter. In April 2009, a year prior to his major label debut, influential rap broadcaster Angie Martinez asked Drake point blank on her show if this was the case, and he replied, "I definitely don't write for Wayne. I'll write with Wayne if we're doing a song together, as far as contributing ideas to each other, but Wayne is a genius." In this same interview he actually attributed Wayne with helping *him* compose his songs.

Lil Wayne was Drake's rap reason for being in many respects. But his role model hit a low on March 2010, when Wayne entered Rikers Island for a one-year sentence for gun possession charges. Following a concert in New York's Beacon Theatre on July 22, 2007, Wayne was arrested for having a .40 caliber gun. Now Drake was not being asked what he was cooking up with his mentor or what remixes he was working on — the focus shifted to how he was coping with having his friend in jail while he was getting set to launch his hotly anticipated CD. In a *Rolling Stone* interview Drake walked readers through the prison visitation ritual he had grown accustomed to. "You get a van to take you over the [Rikers Island] bridge. Then a bus comes to pick you up and takes you in. The bus is full, and people usually trip out when I'm on it. Then I get to go in with Wayne and give him a hug and talk for a couple of hours." The gun possession charges held up in court, but Drake showed a reluctance to believe that his hero was guilty. "In my opinion he didn't do anything wrong," he told CNN. "I think that was the opportunity to make an example out of somebody who didn't deserve to be made an example out of." In full support of his mentor, Drake even wore a "Free Wayne" T-shirt during his performance at the 2010 VH1 Hip Hop Honors awards show. While in Rikers Island jail, Lil Wayne was still able to masterfully record his verses on the Rikers remix of the Drake and Jay-Z collaboration "Light Up" from a telephone within the facility. Wayne and Drake's manager Cortez Bryant broke down how they were able to pull this recording stunt off. "Wayne called [Young Money president] Mack Maine and told Mac to have his engineer set up in the studio," Bryant told reporter Larry Leblanc. "They figured it out over at the Hit Factory, where the phone went straight to the board to record, and it was done. There was a time that he was going to call in, and everybody was ready."

While Drake had grown accustomed to being an opener for A-list American urban music talents (the first time Drake ever traveled to perform overseas it was as a support act for Jay-Z), or performing live concerts in smaller venues, by April 2010 he was a headliner in his own right, inviting Frances and the Lights and k-os along on his Away from Home tour. The tour was to kick off on April 5, 2010, at Slippery Rock University in Pennsylvania and wrap up in Houston on May 20, but then it was extended to include dates throughout Europe to take advantage of the *Thank Me Later* buzz. Prior to the announcement of his tour, Drake had only officially released one single from the upcoming album, the anthemic "Over," which cleverly flips and depoliticizes one of rap group Dead Prez's strongest verses from their classic "It's Bigger Than Hip Hop" song. But at this landmark moment in his career, Drake got the worst possible news a loyal son can get — his mother had become severely ill. Drake postponed his entire European tour. "Despite my best hopes, it is apparent that my mother will need surgery earlier than anticipated," Drake said in a statement. "In light of this news, I have made the difficult decision to cancel my European tour in

Drake at the VH1 Hip Hop Honors: The Dirty South show in his
Free Wayne T-shirt (© Scott Gries/PictureGroup)

order to support her during her recovery, just as she supported me through the years." He ended up rescheduling his headlining shows in London to November 2010 and postponing his other dates.

This was a wake-up call, as there had been moments where Drake had struggled to keep his life balanced and stay connected to his mother. Despite being on the road constantly Drake tried to maintain a solid connection with his mother, texting her frequently while he was on the road. But he confided to MuchMusic host and friend T-RexXx that the demands of the music industry and live concert touring had still disrupted the communication between him and his mom, and that he was not happy about that. Asked about his 2011 New Year's resolutions, he replied, "Going forward, the improvements I want to make are more personal things, like I forgot to call my mom when the clock hit 12, and those types of things are like, ah, man! I can't start the new year off like that." He added, "I took her out to dinner tonight and made up for it as best I could. . . . I gotta be a little more in tune and in touch with my life, and realize that my life and *the* life are not the same thing."

Certainly nothing could have prepared his mother for her son's meteoric rise. "Until that phone call from Lil Wayne, we were pretty much inseparable," she told MTV. But she's grown accustomed to the flurry of activity that had enveloped her son's career over the last few years. "What I've realized is what he's off doing is every parent's dream."

While Drake was enjoying the process of producing his debut CD, he admitted that his mother's health had him preoccupied as much, if not more, than his impending chart success. He said, "And then my family I'm missing like months, shaving off people's lives that you don't know how long they're gonna be around. My mom is sick, so that scares me a lot."

Drake knew that touring was necessary and critical to his success, but getting his bearings in the whirlwind world of dealing with venues and promoters posed some challenges. Drake revealed to MTV how one concert he performed in Atlanta in 2009, which he described as "the most fucked-up performance I've ever done in my life," helped shape how he manages his live concert and touring experience.

While prepping for this particular club concert, his gut told him something wasn't right. "I was nervous because I just walked in and I was like, 'This doesn't look right. Why are we in some weird area with curtains? Where's the stadium? Where's the dressing room? What are we doing?" he said. His lead touring guitar player, Adrian Eccleston, felt that the promoter had oversold the venue. He told MTV that it felt like "there were 1,000 cameras in the front rows" for a "club that maybe holds 400 people max." Drake had problems with the way the sound was set up and his mic was chipping out. The sightlines were awful, so he had to stand on a speaker during the performance so his fans could see him. "It was just so 'hood," he said. When his special guest Birdman came out, his microphone wasn't working. Everything was out of sync, and it felt "like a high school talent show."

The show did go on, but Drake's perfectionist tendencies left him feeling jaded and worn down. "I was just disappointed in a lot of people around me, after we had just taken all of this time to rehearse, and build up this great show, and it's supposed to be so I can shine as an artist. . . . Everyone had time to do everything else but make a good show." Drake was forced to take a strong stand in this instance, to ensure these types of incidents wouldn't happen. "Some people are going to get fired after tonight, I promise you that," he said at the time.

Even an uneventful day on the tour trail can wear down the performer. He described the experience to MTV: "It's that nonstop, you know. You think you're getting sleep, but the sleep you're getting isn't even really real, only 'cause you're just so exhausted that you're catching up to tired. It's just so many different places, shaking so many hands, being around smoke and liquor and bad food. It's interesting, its almost like pushing the human body to its extreme limits." And when you're expected to deliver your first album, that experience becomes even harder. "I'm juggling my album, my reputation as a performer, my health, and my sanity, it escapes me a lot of times, it escapes me how I've even still going," Drake confessed to MTV from inside his tour bus.

Even with the stresses of trying to get *Thank Me Later* completed on a strict schedule, his first real deadline imposed by a major record label, 40 was fully confident in his right-hand rapper's ability to shine, despite what naysayers might have thought. "Nobody believed it was gonna happen," he said. "I was telling people that it was gonna happen, and I believed it enough to quit my day job and spend money I didn't have. . . . Drake is unstoppable because no one can tell him no. You can't tell him no. Because he knows he's got me. And between me and him, we can give you a mastered record. So if he has the ideas and the motivation and I have the means of producing it, it's his ultimate freedom."

By the time Drake made a stop at the University of Missouri in Kansas City on April 26, 2010, most of the audiences he greeted on tour could sing along to his songs, and many fans were uploading his concert clips to YouTube. On this night Drake told the crowd that he would be submitting the final version of *Thank Me Later* right after his performance.

After his important first tour and first album were completed, Drake had enough confidence to tackle new audiences. Right after his headlining tour, many hardcore rap faithful wondered how he ended up on the Bamboozle Festival's line-up, a festival more known for its rock, emo, punk and skater culture–friendly performers than anything. But it was a part of Lil Wayne's master plan to have Drake win over all audiences, regardless of genre, much like he had. In the face of a crumbling business, it made sense — and cents — to go after the broadest audience possible.

As he graduated to stadium-sized crowds, Drake honed his

performing skills to hold the audience's attention while still maintaining a crucial personal connection. "I used to do this thing where I'd rap and I'd look down at the ground and never look at anybody," he admitted of his early days as a live performer. "And everyone used to always talk about it, so I make sure now that I look people in their eyes the entire show. That's my thing now. . . . I want them to know that I'm serious about what I'm saying."

Drake initially gained his rap audience one Myspace friend at a time, and he still tries to treat his fans as individuals. His approach was clearly resonating with fans, and he related, "I got the greatest compliment from somebody at one of the biggest shows, actually. They said to me that in a room of 8,000 people, you make it feel like you're speaking directly to everybody. I don't see it as much more than what I owe them."

As the wider rap community counted down the days until *Thank Me Later* would be released, lucky concertgoers got teasers of the hotly anticipated disc at select live shows, if they happened to be in the right place at the right time. One of the first songs to make it out of his debut was "Fireworks," which leaked on May 26. The song directly addressed the rumored schism between him and Wayne and touched on his rumored dalliance with Rihanna. "I took the time on that song and every single verse to be really honest about questions that I never, ever answer," Drake told *Billboard* about the heartfelt song with the catchy strings and splashy drums. "I guess the sort of fear that me and Wayne will be driven apart by the fact that I actively did gain success as an artist, and I always worry that sometimes that might drive a wedge between us, which I pray it never will and which I say in the song."

The highly anticipated song he'd recorded with rap kingpin Jay-Z, titled "Light Up," leaked as well. Drake didn't seem overly concerned with his songs being shared online, because he was confident in his built-in fanbase's ability to go out and buy the authentic product. After all, with *So Far Gone*, he'd already seen people buy what they could get for free. "If I had put out an album that was poor quality of music that people didn't enjoy, then I think the leaks would hurt me, but really because a lot of the feedback has been great it can only help, word of mouth spreading around," Drake said. And on June 2, 2010, via Twitter Drake reiterated this position. "I gave away free music for years so we're good over here . . . Just allow it to be the soundtrack to your summer and ENJOY! June 15th!"

He may have seemed confident, but beyond the hype and hoopla, pomp and pageantry, deep down he knew he had a long way to go to live up to the advance praise for the leaked songs, the positive news clippings, the premature crowning as rap's new king or the comparisons to his idols Jay-Z and Kanye. On May 27, a few days prior to his leak explanations, Dr. Marc Lamont Hill, a leading hip hop intellectual in the United States, posted a "Why I Hate Drake" blog post, dissecting the Drake phenom and asking some tough questions that few might've had the cojones to ask publicly. Why did he unleash his ire on Drake? "Because he represents several things that I find troublesome about the current mainstream hip hop scene," he wrote. "Instead of relying on his intellectual and artistic gifts, he too often resorts to tired concepts, lazy punch lines and predictable one-liners. This wouldn't be such a problem if he weren't constantly being hailed by the rap world as a dope lyricist rather than what he actually is: a pop song writer. To call Drake an emcee in a world that still includes Black Thought, Lupe Fiasco, Jean Grae, Pharoah Monch or even Eminem is an insult to people who think. In addition to his lyrical deficiencies, there is something naggingly inauthentic about Drake. . . . From his faux-Southern accent to his corporate-funded 'street buzz,' Drake has been perfectly prepped to become hip hop's version of a boy band. Take one look at Drake and you can almost hear the calculations of greedy record execs looking for the next crossover act: Preexisting white fanbase: check. Exotic Ethnic Background: check. Light Skin: check. Celebrity Cosigners: check."

Perhaps feeling that he himself had been prematurely elevated to legendary status, Drake tried to set things straight to *Billboard*. "Legendary status can't be dictated by the people who are still here witnessing it," he said. "Legendary status is when the next generation comes up. The kids that are 15 right now and will be going to college in five or six years — if they say, 'Yo, I remember when Drake came to this school. That's one of the most legendary shows ever,' that's when you're a legend. I'm young. I'm 23. This is too soon. I really want to grow and be that guy."

On June 15, 2010, *Thank Me Later* debuted at number one on the *Billboard* 200 list, selling 447,000 albums, a sliver below gold certification (500,000). It was deemed an undeniable success "thanks to the rich and nuanced production and Drake's thoughtful, playful and intense lyrics" according to Allmusic. Music bible *Rolling Stone* praised his rap flow and delivery, writing that "Drake is in total command of a style that would have been hard to imagine dominating hip hop a few years ago: he's subtle and rueful rather than loud and lively; emotionally transparent rather than thuggy." *Thank Me Later* went platinum in America on July 20, after only five weeks in stores. Drake showed his appreciation for those who supported him on Twitter: "Thank you to everyone who allowed us to go platinum on a debut album! WOW." At the time, *Thank Me Later* boasted the biggest debut week for a solo act's album since Susan Boyle's *I Dreamed a Dream* debuted at No. 1 with 701,000 sales the year prior in November 2009. In the same period, only Sade's *Soldier of Love* — an artist Drake desperately wanted to appear on his own CD — had generated this kind of interest in the urban music scene's court of public opinion, selling 502,000 copies its first week.

The Drake frenzy was only getting started. Just as his buzz was beginning to rise to unprecedented levels, a free concert featuring Drake and pop band Hanson was scheduled to happen on June 15, the day his CD was released, to kick off the annual concert series at the South Street Seaport in Manhattan. A free show featuring the rap artist du jour was sure to bring pandemonium to New York City streets, and that's exactly what happened: an estimated 25,000 people came to the Seaport. Organizers suspected the event might be over-capacity when the hardcore Drake faithful started arriving at the venue early in the day for an evening performance. When almost twice the 10,000 anticipated audience members showed up, it was pure bedlam. Event organizers might have slightly underestimated the drawing power of a bill featuring both Drake and Hanson, especially given the influence of Drake followers on Facebook and Twitter, where the news of the free concert had been buzzing. Drake's CD signing at the Best Buy at Union Square had generated large crowds numbering in the hundreds earlier in the day, but it was nothing like this.

Some photographs of the event show a fan hanging off a Pizzeria Uno restaurant canopy; bottles flew through the air, and fans were crushed in the push toward the stage. Drake had no idea that chaos had erupted. By the time police arrived at the venue, it was way over capacity. Some attendees got arrested for disorderly conduct, others got antsy and tossed chairs. Police even had to spray mace to settle down rowdy troublemakers. The concert was canceled. Drake took to Twitter to give a play-by-play: "Police are shutting down the show at South Seaport! I'm on my way anyways ... Drizzy Hendrix Woodstock 2010." Drake apologized to his supporters. "To all the devoted fans that came out I wish you could have seen what I had planned!" he wrote. "Until next time."

The Seaport riot was reportedly enough to convince the organizers of ABC's *Good Morning America* summer concerts to cancel a July 16 concert possibility in Central Park. The NYPD had communicated the security and safety concerns of hosting Drake. While the series had a track record of booking other chart-topping acts like Miley Cyrus and Alicia Keys, Drake's social media profile had raised the promotional stakes significantly.

Fans crowd at the ill-fated South Street Seaport show (© Leia Jospé)

What do you do if you get so popular your shows get canceled? If you're Drake, you decide to run them yourself, of course. Always business-savvy and in favor of a hands-on approach, the young emcee decided to run his own OVO festival back home in Toronto. He and his team would retain full creative, organizational and fiscal control, guaranteeing proper venues and slick artist lineups with some chemistry. A savvy entrepreneurial gesture, the OVO festival was strategically timed to coincide with arguably the busiest weekend in Toronto for the urban music community. Black music enthusiasts from around the globe looking for Caribbean-based music like calypso and reggae come to Toronto annually during its Civic Holiday long weekend to take in the largest carnival-style event of its kind in North America, Caribana. The OVO festival was smartly set up to feature him performing with a bunch of friends and celebrity guests.

No one could question Drake's popularity at the time, but it was still surprising nevertheless to witness the Molson Amphitheatre, one of the largest concert venues in Toronto, fill up with Drake fans, when essentially every other commercial promoter had music events happening this same weekend. The Caribana weekend is largely viewed as a cash grab for local area music promoters looking to capitalize on 1.2 million people looking for something to do on the four-day weekend.

While hosting his first festival he operated much like a music industry magnate in training would, arranging to share the stage with hip hop royalty — Jay-Z, Eminem, Rick Ross, Young Jeezy and Fabolous. Hardcore rap enthusiasts, who might be less interested in megastars like Eminem, were catered to as well, as he brought out Houston underground rap legend Bun B.

For those naysayers who might've thought that Drake didn't quite respect the Canadian rap canon enough, he had something for them too, bringing Toronto's hip hop ambassador Kardinal Offishal up onstage to get the crowd amped. This gesture and opportunity was offered to Kardinal following an alleged beef between the two camps over authorization of song use. Or the conflict could've just come about because, as Kardinal quipped, "Where we come from there can't be more than one star at the same time unfortunately." Despite some haters' hopes that the two rappers would go at each other's throats in a modern day Ralph Ellisonian Battle Royal format, Kardinal viewed his OVO invite as a genuine burying of any perceived hatchet.

"It was a very good gesture because we were acquaintances from his early stages, before the hype. When they called me to come out and perform 'Ol' Time Killin' — they said that's their favorite Kardi joint of all time — it was a dope gesture in our own way for our city. It was like when Bob Marley brought political rivals Edward Seaga and Michael Manley together at that historic One Love Peace concert in Jamaica, two opposing viewpoints joined hands onstage. This was that for our generation in Toronto. It squashed a lot of the foolishness, and so-called beef. It showed two powerhouses from the city coming together, showing love. Many fans in the city, post-concert, said that was the biggest Toronto unity political statement the city has seen. . . . It was awesome and it was necessary."

Not content to rest on his laurels and celebrate his achievements, among them a platinum-selling debut and a new music festival he operated dominating the headlines, he announced new dates for another headlining tour. When *Thank Me Later* was out for a few months and had made its mark, he began his Light Dreams & Nightmares tour in support of the disc. Drake quite literally turned up the Miami heat when he kicked off his tour at the James L. Knight Center on September 20, and the tour skipped across the country to wrap up November 6 in Las Vegas — a mere two days after his mentor Lil Wayne was to be released from jail. His live show was becoming a full-on production, unlike many hip hop concerts that lack the high-end production values of pop and rock concerts. He was incorporating backing vocalists who could flesh out the sound and adding properly orchestrated lighting schemes into the mix. "This is my first time ever being able to create a world," Drake said.

SEX SYMBOL, RELUCTANT HEART-THROB

Drake's rumored fling with Rihanna was linked to an alleged dust-up with her ex, Chris Brown (© Frank Micelotta/PictureGroup)

New York Times reporter Jon Caramanica once wrote that "no rapper

has been as woman-focused as Drake since LL Cool J." Dissecting

his lyrics, his personal life and persona, that much is clear. "Make Me

Proud," his homage to a mythical ideal woman, offers as much insight

into his view on women as any song. When Drake told *Entertainment*

Weekly openly and honestly that trying to find genuine love is "one

of my worst character traits," he wasn't kidding. "I look for love in

the wrong people," he told *EW*. "It just always seems like the women

I find are poison for me. I love women that can just walk into a room and stop the whole area. And I think that those initial qualities always end up getting me hurt, which is a crazy thing for a guy to say."

Case in point: when Drake released "Miss Me," a less splashy third promotional single from *Thank Me Later*, the song contained some other curious lyrics in reference to a woman named Maliah. The woman in question was later found out to be Maliah Michel, a buxom former stripper. Drake had reportedly met Michel in a strip club. "Drake had actually come to the club where I work in Houston called Dreams," Michel told *Vibe* magazine. "I think that's where he first saw me. I didn't even get to speak to him that night and like a week later everybody started telling me Drake shouted me out in a song." Drake had included her name in the "Miss Me" song lyrics without even knowing her, according to Michel. "I thought that it was so cool because I hadn't even talked to him before. I mean, obviously he saw something he liked. . . . This guy didn't even say anything but gave me props on a song."

Drake was reportedly so smitten that Michel said he called and asked her to star in his "Find Your Love" video. Michel had previously been in videos with R&B superstars Lloyd and Ne-Yo. "I got to admit I was really geeked and could barely talk," she said about Drake's invitation. Despite being seen with Drake at public events (she was allegedly spotted at his CD listening party in Toronto) and their apparent onscreen chemistry, Michel did what most women linked to Drake have done — declare that they are only "good friends." "We like hanging out . . . having fun together," she said when quizzed about their alleged romance. "That's all that anyone needs to know." "Find Your Love" was arguably the most syrupy love ballad written by Drake for wide distribution, and it began to reveal why he devotes much of his recording time to trying to reconcile his feelings toward women.

Women, on the other hand, don't seem too conflicted about him, and taken with his natural good looks and those R&B-influenced

songs, a big part of the reason is style. He's been one of *People*'s Sexiest Men Alive, a *GQ* Man of the Year and has graced *GQ*'s April 2012 Style Bible issue. Like all style originals, Drake wears his clothes with great confidence — he knows how to edit his presentation for maximum effect.

When it comes to fashion and brand building — which includes anything from styling to helping coordinate the OVO clothing line, working on unique merchandising deals (fans could exclusively purchase select OVO merchandise like Swiss army knives, floatable key chains and bottle openers on his Spring 2012 Club Paradise tour) and creating content for the website — Drake relies on Oliver El-Khatib. Bred in Toronto and London, Lebanese-Scandinavian El-Khatib cut his trendsetting teeth working at the now-defunct legendary Toronto Queen Street West clothing store Lounge. Operated by now NYC-based Community 54 clothier Daymon Green, the upscale shop clothed Canadian TV and urban music talents including Juno Award–winning rapper Choclair, and ex-MuchMusic VJs Matte Babel and Master T. Green said El-Khatib has always been "ahead of the curve" and that his "influence is what helps make Drake so different."

"When Oliver was working with us in the early 2000s, around 2003, we always needed someone on the team who isn't a yes man, and he was that guy," said Green, who took the eager teenager with no real fashion background fresh out of high school on as an intern, under the advice of his colleague Joel Reilly. "As a 19-year-old he would be that guy to tell you that something looks wack. That's an important trait to have in this business."

The members of his extended OVO team have been noted for their sartorial splendor, and Green said that Oliver plays a big role in the hip hop fashionista flavor Drake and his team display at public outings and in videos, blending high-end fashion with street sensibilities. "When people are wearing jewelry and XXXL size jersey, a lot of those people were scratching their heads when

Oliver came out with Drake wearing Commes des Garçons and A.P.C. lines, keeping it street, with a fresh pair of Jordans. Even that whole Good Wood trend [wooden fashion accessories], you have to give Oliver and Drake a lot of credit for that, because no one was wearing anything like that for years.... Now it's normal for rappers to be wearing Martin Margiela, Raf Simons. That wasn't looked at as being cool. Now every kid wants to go super high-end designer, and Drake with the help of Oliver has opened the scene up."

This keen fashion sense is why Drake and El-Khatib worked in collaboration with respected expedition outfitter Canada Goose to create limited edition custom-made jackets that are quite costly for your average fashion-conscious youth (the 2011 Chilliwack jacket cost $5,000).

Interestingly, Drake's been noted to have a Bill Cosby–esque sweater fetish. At any one moment in time you can see him sporting anything from cardigan sweaters all the way to thick hooded sweaters. "I like sweaters," he admitted to Vulture.com. "I have a sweater obsession, I guess . . . that's honestly my favorite clothing item."

The combination of this sweater-wearing softer side with his reputation as a suave, clean-cut trendsetter has aligned him with a very female-friendly segment of the rap audience. Once described as a "doe-eyed lover boy who hung out with the bad boys," Drake's playboy persona is a familiar one, recalling Nas, with his bad-boy thug charm, and Tupac, whose good looks and lyrical passion made for a potent combo (both thugs *and* hotties adored him). But what makes Drake altogether different from rap playboys of the past is that his loverboy image is underscored by his open, unflinching respect for the women around him, beginning with the ones who raised him.

The playboy persona exhibited in his music and in some of his real life might've arguably come in some way from his dad, who he described in *Fader* magazine as having an "overcool, Shaft-like

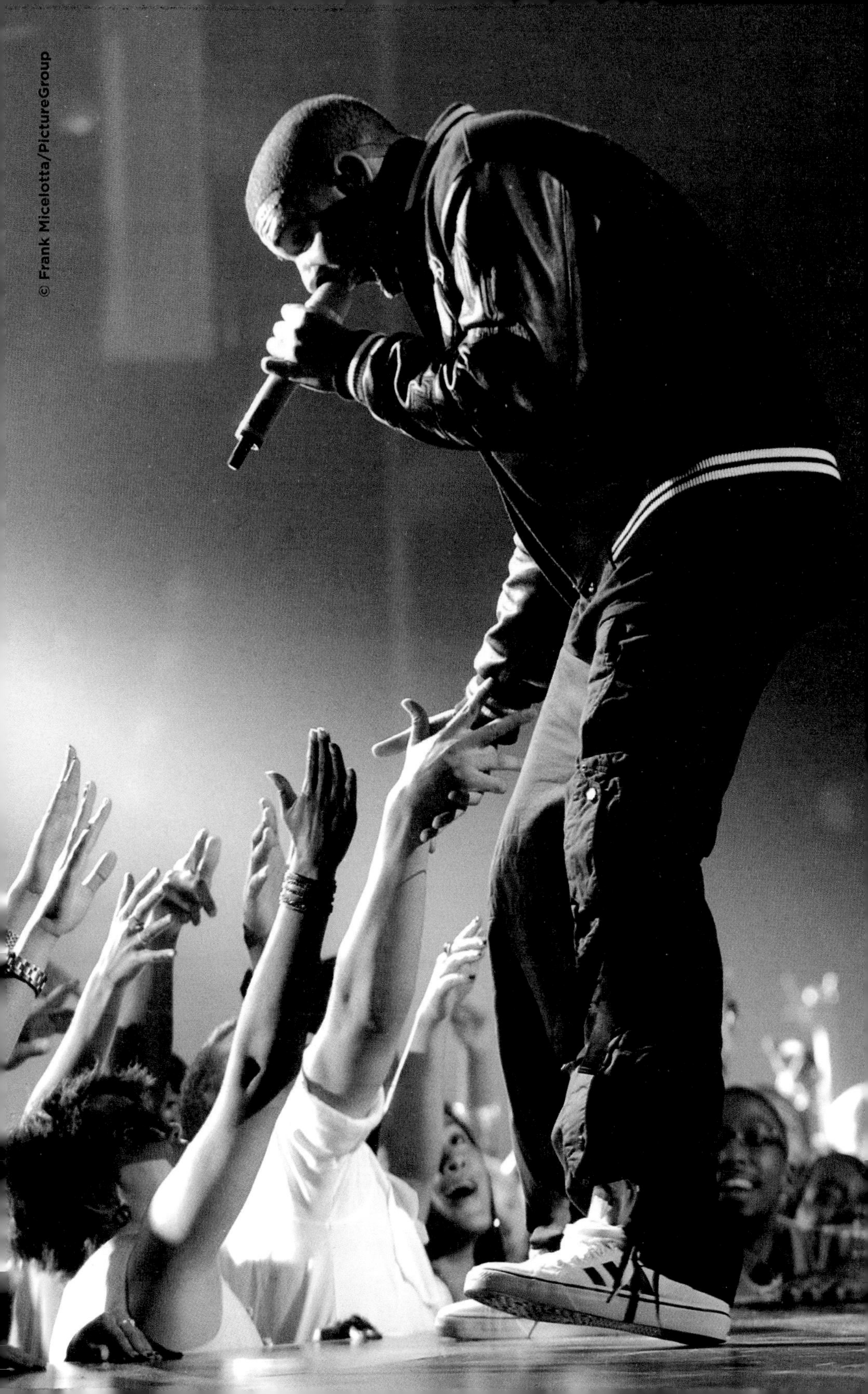

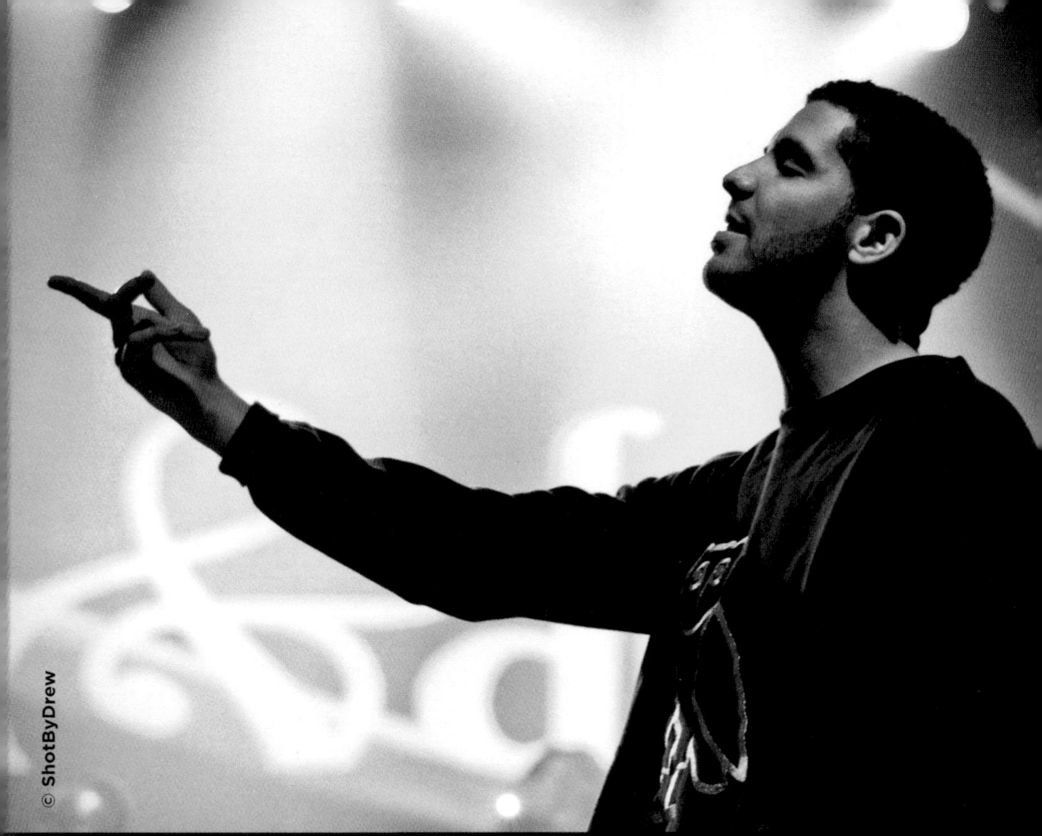

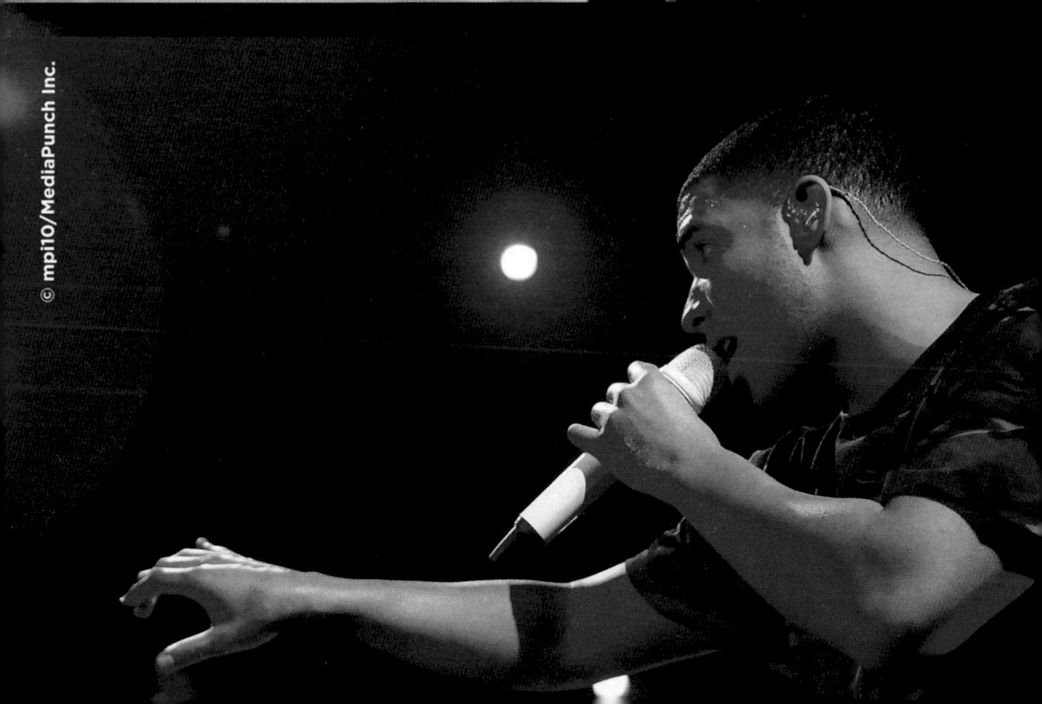

SONGWRITER OF THE YEAR

"FANCY"

"FOREVER"

DRAKE FANCY

FOREVER

ASCAP

2011

MATTHEW "BOI-1DA" SAMUELS

MISS ME

DRAKEOVER

"MISS ME"

"OVER"

SONGWRITER OF THE YEAR

"FANCY"

"MISS ME"

DRAKE FANCY

MISS ME

A S C A P
2011

DRAKEOVER

ALICIA KEYS
UN-THINKABLE (I'M READY)

"OVER"

"UN-THINKABLE
(I'M READY)"

BOI-1DA, DRAKE AND 40

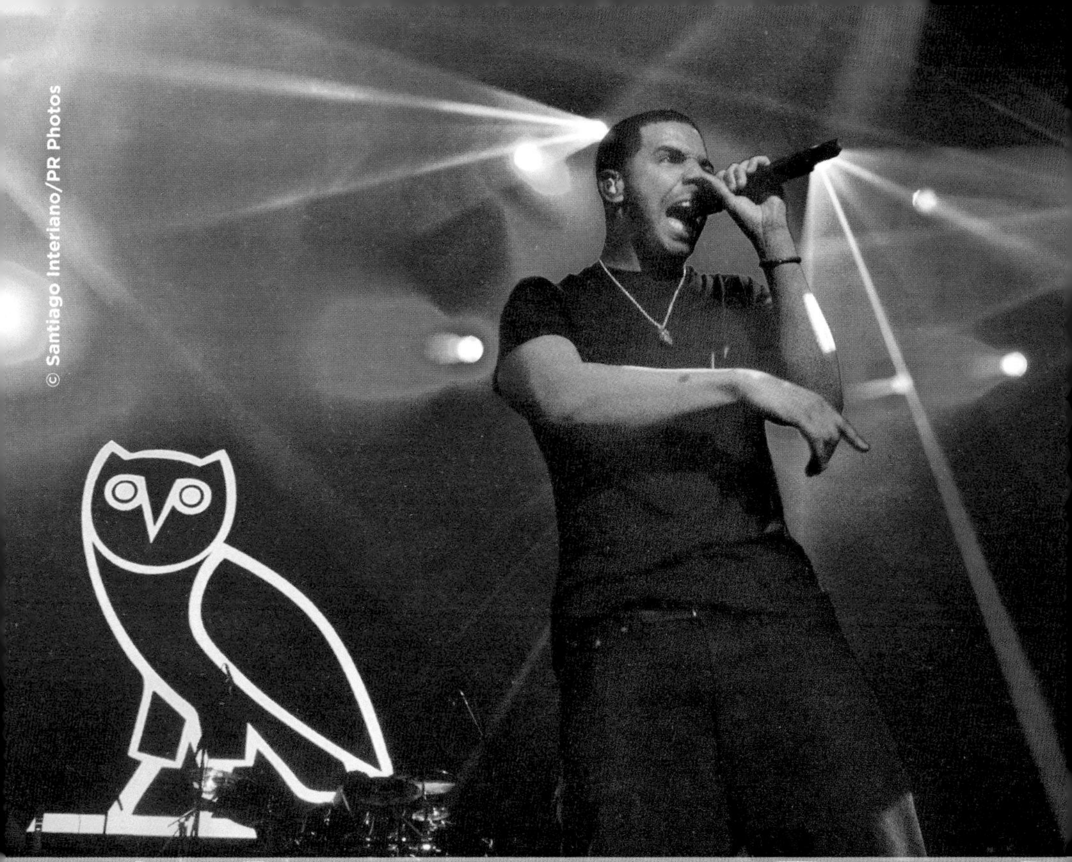

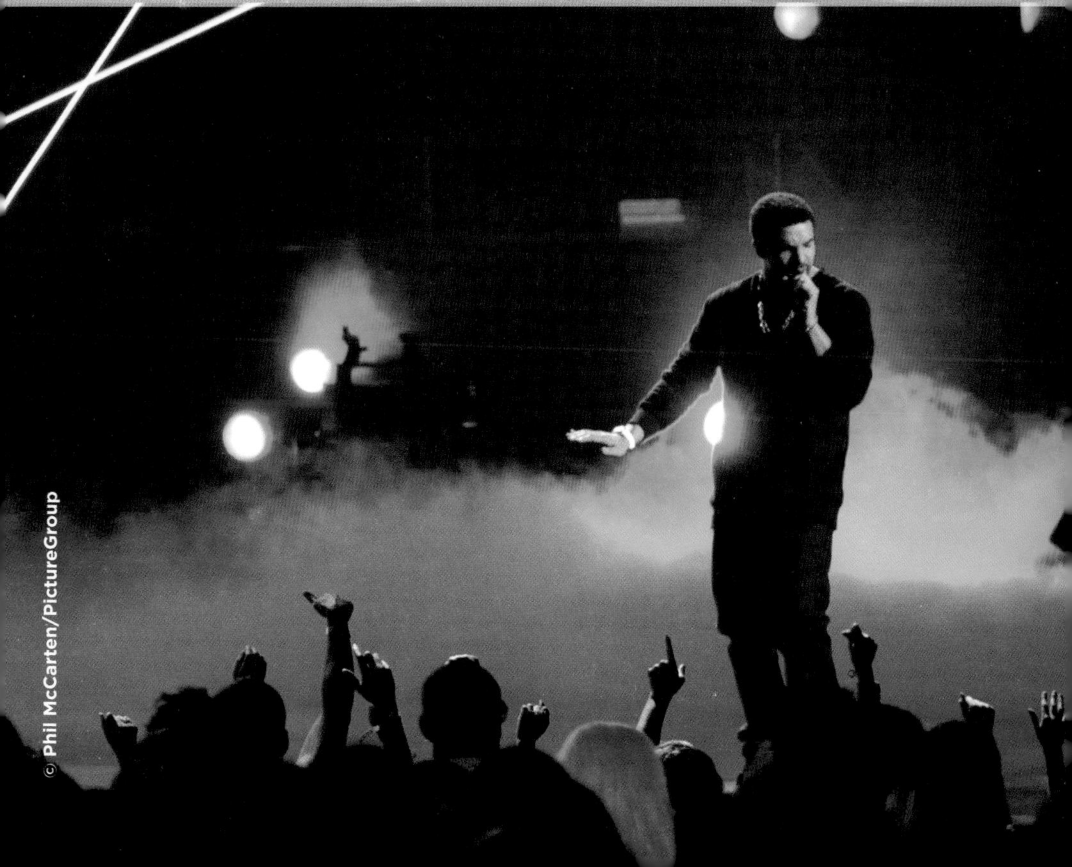

personality." He modestly explained, "I think that I get my charm from my father, if I do have any charm at all." His more sensitive, less brash side comes from hanging around his mother and *bubbe*. "He really did grow up in a very female-oriented household," his mom, Sandi, told MTV. "I don't know, maybe living with a mother has given him that softer side."

Drake still carries around with him the scars of the break-up of his parents, and it informs how he evaluates his current relationships with women over 20 years later. Drake said he learned "what not to do" in a relationship while witnessing his dad's treatment of his mother. "I was there when my mom used to be upset or cry because of the things my father would do," he told *Elle Canada*. "In a rare moment of self-realization, my dad confirmed that I should treat women better." This fragility shows up in signature songs like "Fireworks." By the third verse, Drake addresses his parents' divorce and how he hopes to one day find true love for himself.

In a CNN interview, Drake admitted that his love-afflicted songwriting and videos like "Fancy" (which was shot "to make women feel special," but was never released) are directly influenced by the hold the stronger sex has on his life. "I'm inspired by the woman. I'm inspired by the makeup of a woman," he said. "Their mind, their conversation, the emotions that they exude, that pour out of them. I love women. I love to study women. I'm not a womanizer, but I love to study behavior patterns of a woman, and really how to interact with them, because I like to write for women."

One long-running feature of the Drake concert experience is the female-heavy audiences who show their appreciation to him by tossing their bras. (Tom Jones, eat your heart out.) The bra-tossing at one point became so reliable, that he started to incorporate it into his show. "I put like the biggest breasts' bras on my mic stand," Drake replied when asked by broadcaster Nardwuar about a bra-covered mic stand he had set up at a Cleveland tour stop. "I try and showcase the fact that women with a full chest it's nothing to be ashamed of. You shouldn't go get them reduced. They're beautiful, breasts are a beautiful thing. And I actually have an entire trunk. I think there's about four or five hundred bras in this trunk. It's a black trunk. And I carry it with me on the road. It's pretty much every bra that I've ever received. It's a statement, it's just part of me really embracing women. I love women a lot, man, and I just want them to look up onstage and see pieces of them."

How exactly did he become this modern-day babe magnet? He humbly maintains that women like him because of his music, not his looks. "I don't take my shirt off, I don't pride myself on the physical conditioning aspect of it," Drake said. "But I get onstage and I start singing the words to a song, and they do throw bras and panties. They do cry and faint, and I truly believe it has a lot do with my music." Drake admitted that at one point in his career he felt pressure to have a certain look. "I know there's things about me that I want to change, just because they make me self-conscious," he said. "That's why I get up and I'm pressed to go to the gym because I look at the TV and I see all these dudes with their shirts off, and it makes me self-conscious."

Thrust into the role of teen heartthrob at a young age, it was during his time on *Degrassi* that he developed more swagger and confidence in dealing with the opposite sex. "*Degrassi* was some wild times," admitted Drake, "but things have gotten to the point where I can create my own pandemonium . . . it's a little more exciting now because it's like beautiful, grown women. Women I'd actually want to date."

The vast majority of the women Drake's been linked to have been black women. One of Drake's first significant teen fling relationships with someone of a similar profile came when he dated Canadian R&B songstress Keshia Chanté. This was before Aubrey Graham became Drake. He said that she was "one of the first people in the industry I met and we just connected." When quizzed about this alleged tryst by MuchMusic VJ Sarah Taylor, Drake replied,

"Uh, I guess. Sure, why not? At a young point in my life, when I was young," then added, "sure, I would be proud to call her [ex]. She's a cool person. I'd be proud to say that we had our time when we were like 16 years old." In a later interview with MuchMusic, Keshia Chanté reluctantly came clean about the impact Drake had on her life romantically. "I will love that man unconditionally for the rest of my life," she said. "He knows what it is. We have history. I've known him since I was a little girl. We just have a love/hate relationship, so I prefer to love him from afar."

While Drake has been romantically linked to many women — death, taxes and Drake dating rumors are but a few things we can expect with some certainty — there's one particular woman who formed his ultimate hottie composite, a woman he uses as a reference point for his current love interests. And her name is Pam Grier. Widely known as a '70s blaxploitation cinema star who almost single-handedly popularized a largely niche film genre with her looks, charm and bombast, Grier is the one woman who he admits made him go weak in the knees growing up. "I think Pam Grier is really responsible for shaping my taste in women if you really look at her," he confessed.

While some pop personalities might not be so quick to tweet or rhyme off during an interview what women they obsess about publicly, Drake tends to have little problem broadcasting his celebrity crushes to the world. Many of these crushes interestingly involve older women ("I like older women, period," he said). Meagan Good is one woman he fantasized about when he was a teenager. "When I was 17 I used to watch anything that Meagan Good was in," he related. "I remember I met her one time, and I thought for sure I made a lasting impression. And then I saw her again and I was like, 'Whassup' . . . she didn't remember me at all. *At all.* It was so embarrassing."

Arguably, his most open significant crush involves British soul crooner Sade, who he always has nothing but flattering things to say about. Drake tried to get her to record with him on *Thank Me Later*, with no success (though his producer 40 did get a piece of the legend, remixing her "The Moon and the Sky" song featuring Jay-Z). While he was trying to court her publicly to record with him for his debut, he told MTV, "Sade not only embodies a lot of class, her brand is so strong and she's such an amazing woman, but the melody she chooses to use and her voice has that dark, sexy feel that a lot of *So Far Gone* has," Drake explained. "When Sade's 'King of Sorrow' comes on, you feel it, consistently. So I just want to try to experiment and see if there's a way to bring her into the hip hop world."

During this public courting ritual, Sade, who had just released her 10th album, *Soldier of Love*, after a decade-long hiatus, wasn't planning to take Drake up on his offer anytime soon. "I don't think they have contacted me," Sade explained to the *National Post*. "I've never collaborated because I've always avoided working outside my safety zone — I can be exactly who I am and can fail or succeed within the moment. I feel safe working like I do. I wouldn't want to work in a situation where I am expected to deliver, because I think I wouldn't deliver."

Drake eventually addressed the snub and said he hoped to one day collaborate with Sade. "I personally feel we could have done something amazing. But I don't think she really knows who I am, really, my genre of music. I put it out there. It was more of a hopeful thing. It was a very early stage where I was at when I said that I was hoping. One day."

Due to the rapid ascent of Drake's career, and the accompanying paparazzi frenzy, it has been hard for many Drake fans and non-fans alike to distinguish between who he actually dated, and what has become tabloid fodder. For example, Drake's relationship with pop star Rihanna toed that line. Neither Drake nor Rihanna said they were an item — though Drake replied to *XXL* magazine that the idea of him dating Rihanna was "semi-true." But when asked about this alleged celebrity romance, he was quick to dispel these rumors. "Just good friends" was the relationship status he offered on the red carpet at the 2009 MuchMusic Video Awards.

Rihanna was asked pointedly about her situation with Drake by broadcaster Angie Martinez. "We weren't really sure what it was," she said of their rumored dalliance. "We just went out — my friends, his friends. I definitely was attracted to Drake, but I think it is what it is, like it was what it was. We didn't want to take it any further. It was at a really fragile time in my life, so I just didn't want to get too serious with anything or anyone at that time." Drake on the other hand might've viewed their tryst in a different way. "I was a pawn. You know what she was doing to me?" he told the *New York Times*. "She was doing exactly what I've done to so many women throughout my life, which is show them quality time, then disappear. I was like, 'Wow, this feels terrible.'"

He later expanded to *Elle* magazine on the emotional impact her alleged treatment had on his younger fragile psyche. "At the time it hurt, but she didn't mean to. . . . That was the first girl with any fame that paid me any mind. You spend days reading about this person in magazines. All of a sudden you have this number-one song and you're at some birthday party and there she is. And you're just some naive kid from Toronto staying in some shitty-ass hotel who got invited to this party on a whim. That's just how it happened." While they've moved on from their rumored past, their friendship has remained intact, and their professional relationship secure and successful. In Rihanna's "What's My Name?" Drake provides the catchy guest rap and appears as her love interest in the sultry video, while Rihanna returned the favor, vocalizing on the Jamie xx and Gil Scott-Heron dance remix title track of Drake's sophomore release *Take Care*. On June 13, 2012, an incident at a New York City nightclub between Drake's and Chris Brown's camps — which left Brown with a cut-up chin and innocent bystander Tony Parker, of the San Antonio Spurs, with eye injuries — was allegedly linked to the two stars' feud over Rihanna.

Drake had already gained valuable experience in how to manipulate tabloids and bloggers seemingly obsessed with his love life when he and labelmate Nicki Minaj pulled off a successful faux Twitter marriage in June 2010. The Twitterverse lit up with news that Drake and Nicki Minaj were finally getting married. Many broadcast outlets tried to confirm the news. Drake tweeted, "Please refer to @nickiminaj as Mrs. Aubrey Drake Graham and dont stare at her too long. She's finally mine. :)" Nicki Minaj tweeted back, "Yes, its true. Drake and I tied the knot." After a few minutes of this back-and-forth banter, many thought this hip hop power couple was not entirely outside the realm of possibility.

A day later, the jig was up. Minaj tweeted, "My husband Drake

Cash Money labelmates Nicki Minaj and Drake are widely considered to be the future of urban music (© Frank Micelotta/PictureGroup)

and I have decided to have our marriage annulled. We'll maintain joint custody. Luv, HB." Who were they sharing custody of? "All our SONS," replied Minaj to fan inquiries. It seemed like the prank had gotten way out of control, even affecting Drake's mom. "My mom was actually like, 'What happened? How did you elope?'" he said. Nicki Minaj also went into damage-control mode when she called DJ Drama on Atlanta's Hot 107.9. "Drake is just my little brother, and I kid with him all the time," she said. "We were just being crazy. I think we were a little bit bored. I wouldn't say we were bored; I would say we were being mischievous." Regardless of their marital statuses and pranks, Drake and Minaj have always been great buddies. And the joke was clearly on the bloggers and tabloid crowd.

Drake has had a love/hate relationship with the same Twitter and Tumblr vehicles that helped grow his reach. Later, in November 2011, he told the Source, "Instead of kids going out and making their own moments, they're just taking these images and living vicariously through other people's moments. . . . It's scary, man, simulation life that we're living." He started to look at Twitter differently when his mother Sandi was really ill and going under the knife for surgery. It was one particular, ignorant tweeter who really annoyed him. "My mom was getting surgery and someone came on Twitter and they were like, 'Yo, Drake, I hope your mom dies.'"

Drake has always been able to take these negative energies and convert them into positive or comedic ones, like when in a 2011 appearance on *Jimmy Kimmel Live!*, he and Kimmel debuted a satiric "Tweet, Tweet" rap video they composed on the fictional Twit Records. Dedicated to U.S. President Barack Obama, it parodied the importance and attention given to celebrity tweets. Both rapped about how celebrity tweets largely and sadly dictate the direction society goes in, referencing in their rhymes ex-CNN broadcaster Larry King, Justin Bieber, Shaquille O'Neal, Michael Jordan, Demi Lovato, Tila Tequila and notorious tweeters Ashton Kutcher and Paris Hilton.

As for Drake's current love life, this much is clear. He seems to have overcome the urge he once had to bed as many women as possible, like his A-list rap peers. "I just need something else," he told a *GQ* reporter of the emptiness he felt after a romantic romp. "The seconds after a man reaches climax, that's like the realest moment of your life. If I don't want you next to me in that 15, 20 seconds, then there's something wrong."

Until Drake officially ties the knot, he will be linked to any woman who's near him, who's breathing beside him. To date he's been linked to a bunch of women from Toronto (Jade Lee, Nebby, *Degrassi* alum Andrea Lewis) to American mega-celebs (Serena Williams, Tyra Banks, Quincy Jones's daughter Rashida Jones) and British ones too (R&B star Rita Ora), in addition to a wide assortment of other hotties (Bria Myles, Vanessa Veasley, Teyana Taylor, Kandice Henry, Dollicia Bryant). But Drake's one constant relationship is with his female fans, who regardless of his public affairs, continue to be wooed by the man and his music.

JUNO
DISS?

In a daring move by CARAS (the Canadian Academy of Recording Arts and Sciences organization, which administers the Junos), Drake was hired to be the on-air host for the 40th edition of the Junos. It was noteworthy for a few good reasons, one being that this was the first time a Canadian rapper had been granted an opportunity to host the show. To many Canadian urban music enthusiasts this Drake-as-host gesture meant hip hop's time had finally come in Canada.

When Drake announced to the world that he had accepted the Junos hosting gig, it might've been an easy decision to make. Sure, it'd be tough to match the sheer entertainment value of having one of the world's finest comedians like Russell Peters, a former DJ and hip hop junkie who'd hosted the awards in 2008 and 2009, but it was an opportunity for Drake to develop his brand even further. For CTV, the Junos' broadcaster, the decision would have been an easy one. Drake was a good zeitgeisty pick, considering he had millions of Twitter followers who just might tune in and drive the ratings through the roof. Both sides had something to gain from this alliance.

As Drake said, "I want to bring a youthful energy to the show and encourage people to be excited about what Canadian music has to offer." No one knew how the show would go, but by the end of the night, the decision to cast Drake as the show's host was a gamble that paid off. His charisma shone bright and the show ran smoothly. The Junos got venerable news anchor Lloyd Robertson to call Drake "Drizzy" and "homey" during the opening skit, which also featured Justin Bieber and gave the pair the chance to show-case their long-brewing bromantic chemistry. According to Bieber, these two had built up a camaraderie after they met hanging out in similar music industry circles. "Basically, he's from Canada, and we met through mutual people and became homies," remarked Bieber to *Complex* magazine. Shortly thereafter Drake appeared in Justin Bieber's breakout "Baby" video because "he wanted to show love."

This unique ebony and ivory coupling operated in parallel pop culture universes. While the raucous nation of Beliebers had been growing steadily since 2009, the Drake Nation had been catching up. Both entertainers are from southern Ontario, have debuted at number one on the U.S. *Billboard* charts and are largely by-products of the impact of the world wide web, where they first gained their music reputations. They've guest-appeared at each other's concerts (Drake even appears on "Right Here" on Bieber's *Believe*), duelled at awards shows (at the 2010 Junos Drake defeated Bieber in the New Artist of the Year category, while Bieber defeated Drake for Best New Artist at the 2010 MMVAs) and cross-promoted each other's artistic output (Drake showed up on the red carpet at the 2011 Toronto premiere of Bieber's 3D *Never Say Never* concert film, while Bieber tweeted excerpts from Drake rhymes to his 10 million followers in March 2011).

Their two worlds were so intertwined, that by the time these two were the stars of the opening skit at the Juno Awards in 2011, they both even shared a loss at the 2011 Grammy Awards in the Best New Artist category. They were denied the gilded gramophone by the less populist jazz bassist and chanteuse Esperanza Spalding, despite both of them being viewed by many critics as shoo-in favorites to take home the gilded gramophone statuette.

While the previous year at the Junos Drake had taken home New Artist of the Year and Rap Recording of the Year, this year was to be his coming-out party as he had arrived at the show with a leading six nominations. A few of the categories seemed an easy win, especially given that he was a rare Canadian *Billboard* chart-topper who was also respected by critics. (Nickelback, he is not.) When the Best Rap Award was handed out to Shad, the country let out a collective gasp. How could this be? Shad was a very talented and respected rapper, but Drake dominated the North American rap scene on all fronts.

When the awards wrapped up, Drake was zero for six. Completely shut out. To make matters worse, no urban, rap or R&B music artist was even granted an opportunity to perform live at the show that ran over two hours. This was all happening at a time when other urban music talents like Drake's former Renaissance bandmate Melanie Fiona was enjoying great success in the U.S.A., flaunting a 2011 Grammy nomination for her work on John Legend's collaboration with the Roots, *Wake Up!*.

It was a blackout.

No one in any position of authority in the broader Canadian music industry took public umbrage with CARAS, the organizers of the Junos or the Juno rap committee jury members, which was interesting considering what happened in the U.S. with the Grammys when Spalding beat Bieber and Drake. In the U.S. it became front-page news, and influential long time marketing/music exec Steve Stoute took out full page ads in the *New York Times* decrying the decision and arguing that the "awards show has become a series of hypocrisies and contradictions." In it, he severely criticized the Grammys, the show's parent organization the National Academy of Recording Arts and Sciences (NARAS) and its president, Neil Portnow, for missing the boat on Eminem, Kanye and Bieber.

On the one hand, some, like the *Toronto Star*'s Ben Rayner, argued that it made sense that a genuine respected underdog rap talent like Shad could defeat Drake in a Juno Awards show that sometimes gets criticized for awarding top-selling discs released by major labels as opposed to awarding discs with the highest artistic integrity. He wrote that Shad's win over Drake "gave everyone a pleasant surprise" because his disc came "without a shred of the hype or the all-points, big-budget rollout that helped push *Thank Me Later* to the top of the charts." He added, "Shad's win is one of those little triumphs that keeps serious music going at functions like the Junos." The strongest negative responses to Drake being shut out came from people in the Canadian rap community that shared a similarly strained history with the Junos like Kardinal Offishall, a wily veteran, who critics in the rap community thought had been denied Juno Awards in the past for political reasons (like in 2002, when he was the clear favorite, but eventually lost to Swollen Members). He had also witnessed Juno boycotts from other rap acts (the Rascalz, a group he had worked with, actually turned down their Junos in 1998, citing racism and bad politics). He addressed Drake's shut out, touching on the shaky history black music practitioners have had with the slow-moving music bureaucracy in Canada, and the Junos in particular: "The whole purpose of that night itself was to acknowledge and recognize artists for the great efforts that they put forth. For somebody to do what he did, and not win an award?

I don't know what the reason for that is. There's been nobody from this country for hip hop, that did as much as he did up to that point, so I don't know how you don't give him one. At least one? I have no idea. It was an unfortunate unfolding of events, but he handled himself well." His commentary to Toronto-area media about the wider question around the treatment of urban music in particular in Canada was widely circulated, starting an honest discussion about how Canada views black music.

He proclaimed that the Juno Awards showed "utter disrespect" to Drake and urban music in Canada, elaborating, "Unfortunately, this is the good ol' Canadian system that we have here, where they think somehow that's possibly acceptable."

Justin Bieber and Drake, both Ontario bred, dominate music headlines
(© Robin Wong/PR Photos)

Was Rayner right about Shad's win being a good thing, lending credibility to awards shows like the Junos who sometimes come under fire for being too commercial and out of touch with contemporary music realities? (An electronic music category was only added in 2011, while the Grammys have acknowledged electronica since 2005, fusing it with the dance category.) Or was Kardinal onto something? This was the first time in the 40-year history of the Juno Awards that a musician who agreed to host the show and had nominated music didn't win at least one award. When acts like Nelly Furtado, Shania Twain and Céline Dion hosted the Junos, they won 12 awards combined.

While Drake didn't speak publicly about the surprising shut out, you could plainly see the disappointment on his face at what was supposed to be his Juno celebration party at downtown Toronto's Muzik nightclub. Instead his fans spoke for him, some rappers even recording tracks expressing their dismay. Local area hip hop organizer, critic, rapper and superfan Mindbender (Adhimu Stewart) recorded a scathing dub plate rebuke to awards shows like the Junos titled "Utterly Disrespectful." Recorded over Drake's "9 a.m. in Dallas" instrumentals, the song reads like a celebration of Drake's success. And there was no one better qualified to weigh in on the Canadian rap nation and how its heroes were being treated than Mindbender, who's attended (or performed at) so many events that he's widely considered Toronto's unofficial rap mayor. Even Drake acknowledges his influence and presence in Canadian hip hop. "I think Mindbender has been at every single thing that I've ever done in Toronto," Drake told Narduwar during a candid interview. "Mindbender is probably the most avid hip hop head I've ever known in my entire life, and he cares about Toronto hip hop, and Canadian hip hop, I think more than anybody.... That's a guy who really lives it."

On the song, Mindbender rhymed, "It was a whole new low to use dude as the host of the 40th anniversary show yo ... Six nominations and no Juno?" and "Drake still did a great job as master of ceremonies/Put a brave face on to celebrate an industry where half its captains are very phony."

Mindbender recorded his Juno-trashing song after being at the ceremony and witnessing the alleged snub up close and personal, then reading Kardinal Offishall's comments on how the Drake snub was "utterly disrespectful." "An entire show, no rap performance, no urban music performers. He didn't win anything, it seemed like he had been used," remarked Mindbender, who added that the Juno afterparty hosted by Drake at Muzik nightclub in downtown Toronto "was one of the most surreal experiences I ever had in Toronto music history." Describing the party, he noted, "It's an enormous club, there's maybe 3,000 people in there, chandeliers, bottle service, and its set up for a Drake Juno afterparty victory celebration, right? And everyone's standing there in shock. 'He didn't win anything? Is this real?' Drake entered the venue, and thanked people for supporting him. But it was bittersweet."

As for the "Utterly Disrespectful" song itself, no one from Drake's camp had issued a public remark about its content. "I thought it was fitting to record the track on Drake's '9 a.m. in Dallas' beat, the one song that didn't make *Thank Me Later*, a banging Boi-1da creation," explained Mindbender, who started out his rap career rhyming with his identical twin brother Conspiracy as part of the Supreme Being Unit duo. "The song wasn't a disrespect to any of the other Canadian emcees, it wasn't like Shad shouldn't have won the Juno rap award. But Drake should have won something as well. I had to reference the Rascalz situation of turning down the Junos years earlier in the song, because its seemed like we had reverted right back to that."

Despite being hailed by the rap community as the people's champ, Drake's award show history was carrying some weird karma. At the BET Awards six months later, he was called up onstage to pick up the Coca-Cola Viewers' Choice Award on behalf of Rihanna because he guest-rapped on her catchy "What's My

Name?" But in a strange twist of fate, the host had called the wrong name and the winner was actually Chris Brown. Drake went up onstage to accept the award, and then later had to return it. This wasn't the first time that those in the Drake Nation had cringed on his behalf, nor would it be the last. At the 2012 Junos, Drake was again favored to win one of the big awards, like Album of the Year. This time pundits suggested that the fix was in, as he lost the award to a Christmas album of covers recorded by Michael Bublé. A Christmas covers CD? After the Bublé win, Toronto dance music artist Deadmau5 remarked, "That must have been one hell of a Christmas album," while *Now* magazine's Benjamin Boles wrote an op-ed questioning whether this win was a part of an April Fool's joke. Spinner website reporter Joshua Ostroff joined the chorus of Drake supporters, writing, "Drake's loss to a Christmas album is as egregious as Kanye West not being nominated for a best album Grammy for *My Beautiful Dark Twisted Fantasy*," and argued that Drake might not have attended the awards "sensing this impending award show trainwreck." (In the end, Drake did take home Rap Album of the Year, even if it was a poor consolation prize.)

Luckily, from the beginning DIY Drake has insisted that the mainstream music industry wasn't an essential authority. In 2009, *XXL* magazine, the bible of hip hop culture, left him out of their influential 2009 Freshmen 10 issue, instead including lesser-known talents like Charles Hamilton, Wale and others like Mickey Factz, who have yet to make one iota of the splash Drake had. When asked point blank by a *Peace* magazine reporter whether he thought *XXL* magazine had overlooked his talents, he offered up a response rooted in diplomacy. "Nah, the guys they selected were great and had a phenomenal year," he replied, not wanting to offend a periodical that might play a significant role in his career at some point. "I don't consider myself part of any group, because I have a completely different story, and a different approach to this whole thing. Being separate from the pack is actually a positive thing for me."

REPPIN' TORONTO WORLD- WIDE

When Drake crooned on DJ Khaled's 2011 summer anthem "I'm on One" that the only things he cared about were money and his hometown, he wasn't kidding. These shout outs to Toronto date back to "Ransom" and "Successful," but was Drake's success enough for that respect to be reciprocated by an indifferent Canadian music industry infrastructure more interested in supporting indie-rock and pop? While the jury is out on whether Canada can produce another Drake, this much is clear: there are two significant time periods used to label the local Toronto rap scene — B.D. (Before Drake) and A.D. (After Drake).

Hip hop notwithstanding, few Toronto-based bands, in any genre, have been able to make a big splash internationally when coming out as unsigned, independent entities like Drake did. When independent bands like Broken Social Scene opened up American ears to what was happening in Canada's indie music scene with their 2002 commercial breakthrough release *You Forgot It in People*, many bands believed they could also do it big their own way. More recently, Toronto hardcore punk outfit Fucked Up topped *Spin* magazine's 2011 Album of the Year list with *David Comes to Life*, and their seminal 2008 release *The Chemistry of Common Life* got their music added to influential *Pitchfork* playlists. Their headway made it seem possible to be independent-minded, based in Toronto *and* be well known in the U.S. and abroad. But they are not hip hop acts, and before Drake there really was no independent hip hop musician in the history of the form in Canada who could relate to this narrative of being unsigned and blowing up in the U.S. As Fucked Up's Damian Abraham remarked, "Regardless what people say about Drake, watching that guy blow up is really fun because that's never happened to a Canadian hip hop artist." Others like buzzy Toronto electro rap scenesters the Airplane Boys, who have toured with Snoop Dogg and were included in a 2012 *Toronto Life* magazine round up of the "next wave" of Drizzyesque rap exports, have commented that Drake's success is the measuring stick of where the local rap scene was, where it is now and where it needs to be. "You gotta look at Toronto, a couple of years ago, there wasn't a real infrastructure, people didn't believe in the music coming out of here, in terms of the hip hop," related Bon Voyage of the Airplane Boys. "Drake broke barriers out from that kind of mold. . . . He inspired the city a great deal, and rebranded himself to bring our sounds to the world in a way that you can look at Toronto now as a place on the map."

Toronto-born, New York–based producer Marco Polo, who boasts production credits with Kool G Rap, KRS-One and Pharoahe

Monch, views Drake's unusual break out moments as what many expats who had to leave their city to get bigger opportunities dreamed of. "Drake's success I think it's inspiring, you know," said Polo, who's been based in Brooklyn for the last decade. "The way I look at it is, if he's putting the microscope on our city and our country for people to really start checking for us, that's always a positive thing. People are now looking at our scene a bit heavier: it never happened on that level before."

Truly, Drake is Canada's first chart-topping A-list international hip hop star. (Many cite Snow, whose single "Informer" shot to the top of the *Billboard* charts in 1992, as the first, but he was a dance hall singjay, not a rapper, and is largely considered a one-hit wonder now.) Pre-Drake, Kardinal Offishall is considered the next closest thing to an internationally known rapper. Really, the only other Canadian urban music industry export to make major waves in the United States like Drake wasn't even a musician, but a video director named X (Julien Christian Lutz), who directed Drake's edgy "HYFR (Hell Ya Fucking Right)" video. Since 2000, Toronto-bred X has been noted for his visually distinctive music videos, commandeering the respect of America's urban culture elite, much like Drake does now. X has helmed videos for many of the same A-list rap and R&B talents that Drake has collaborated with musically, including Jay-Z, Kanye West, Nicki Minaj, Rihanna, Alicia Keys and Usher.

For most black music practitioners, Drake has become the closest thing to that long imagined Toronto rap ideal. Legends like Dr. Dre, Stevie Wonder and Jay-Z have collaborated with him, despite Drake being rooted in a city where a legitimate hip hop economy and infrastructure doesn't even exist. And it's arguable that Drake's industry clout has more or less helped leverage Toronto into becoming a quasi–hot spot for potential urban music chart-toppers. A few new and notable Toronto-bred acts have begun to leave their mark on both global and western music constituencies: notably K'naan, whose "Wavin' Flag" single was an unofficial

World Cup soccer anthem that charted at number one in more than 20 countries, and The Weeknd, whose dreamy take on R&B dominated critics' best of 2011 lists.

Does Drake's success mark a Toronto rap renaissance that will have talent scouts, agents, music bookers and eager A&Rs rummaging around Drake's hometown of almost six million, seeking the next big thing? When rap icon Raekwon, an integral member of hip hop's greatest group of all time, Wu-Tang Clan, decided to open up his first record label imprint, Ice H2O, in Toronto in fall 2011, it was viewed as an opportunity for American music business impresarios to tap into an untapped rap resource and support acts that never seemed to get the right shot at global stardom. "Hearing

Drake embraces fellow Canadian K'naan at the 2010 Juno Awards
(© Robin Wong/PR Photos)

about all this talent, and no one getting an opportunity? That's spiritual for me," Raekwon told Toronto's *Now* magazine. "It gives me a sense of direction to learn about what's working and what isn't. This is the city I chose to pay homage to." This was a big move coming from a rapper who honestly admitted his knowledge of Canada in general was rooted in crude stereotypes. "We grew up thinking about Canada like there's bears up there, log cabins," he admitted to the *National Post*, "but it's not like that. Toronto's a real city and they respect people who understand the streets and understand the business."

The tale of most Canadian rap and/or R&B success stories has been one of spending long periods of time trying to generate interest locally, nationally and internationally while being virtually ignored by rock 'n' roll obsessed A&Rs, and then being *discovered* by someone from elsewhere. Much like Raekwon's current signing and championing of Toronto rap talent JD Era (who, coincidentally, was a member of the short-lived Toronto underground rap crew The Wise Guys alongside Drake, Bishop Brigante, Johnny Roxx, Ken Masters and Young Tony), when Michie Mee, Canada's queen of rap, was burning up the underground music circuit and became the first Canadian rapper to land a recording contract, it was an American company, First Priority, that had the foresight to sign her. "The more business gets involved with true talent out here [Canada], the more you will see us on front pages and stages," she says point blank. Canada's failure to recognize and support its own talents was a familiar pattern: take Maestro (formerly Maestro Fresh-Wes), whose 1989 chart-busting "Let Your Backbone Slide" remained the top-selling Canadian rap single for 20 years; the influential Dream Warriors, whose 1991 game-changing debut *And Now the Legacy Begins* is one of the finest jazz-influenced rap LPs of all time; the genre-blurring, Grammy-nominated k-os; or Kardinal Offishall — they were all first signed to major American and/or international recording contracts. There are certainly other hugely talented Canuck rap talents who have Canadian recording contracts: Shad has a deal with Black Box Music, but he still has yet to make any real measurable impacts outside of the country.

The history of modern Canadian R&B and soul music tells the same sad story. Mega-sellers from Deborah Cox (at 14 weeks her 1998 song "Nobody's Supposed to Be Here" held the record for longest-running number one single on *Billboard*'s R&B/Hip Hop Songs chart for nearly eight years) all the way through to Grammy-winning SRC/Universal Motown/Roc Nation vocalist Melanie Fiona have had to get out of Dodge to find their own success. "I think it's very specific to certain types of music," Fiona told AUX TV of this disturbing ages-old neglect of black music genres. "Indie rock bands, they have no problems. They're gigging all the time here. I just think that in terms of the market and demographic, there probably needs to be industry-wise a better infrastructure to support the different genres that are popping up from Canada."

With too few urban radio outlets and latent racism in Canada's music industry, Drake's rapid rise to the top of America's charts had no homegrown support, as many label heads and journalists in Canada didn't pick up on Drake until after he got a stamp of approval from American media types.

Strangely, some of the age-old neglect of Canada's urban music talents not only came from the oppressive anti-black music stance of major music labels, but a local rap community that sometimes struggles to support its own talents. Toronto rapper Theology 3 nicknamed his city "Screwface Capital" to describe a scene where locals show indifference or even hostility to their peers' musical output, preferring to look elsewhere for hip hop inspiration, even to this day — despite Drake's astronomical success. "What Drake has done is create a sense of opportunity and hope," he said. However he points out that while audiences "are rooting for the next international breakthrough to come from here, problem is they'll likely miss a number of other dope local acts in the process."

In his song "The Exquisite," well-known local broadcaster and part-time emcee Arcee even suggests that fickle Toronto audiences would pay to go to a concert just to heckle a rapper they didn't like. Drake's enormous success, support of local area producers and overall nice-guy demeanor has done much to counteract this hostility. Drake has been *hard* to hate.

Award-winning Toronto rapper D-sisive eloquently expressed the odd duality perhaps felt by his local rap peers, growing up in a rap scene that eats its young. "No one ever puts it out there. If you're from Canada, Toronto specifically, you cannot look me in the eye or look yourself in the mirror and say you are not jealous of Drake. I am INCREDIBLY jealous of Drake," he admitted to the Toronto Standard website. "But at the same time, I think he deserves it. You're out of your fucking mind if you think otherwise, because this is a talented man who played his cards right."

Certainly, without the success of a Maestro or his successor Kardinal Offishall, who created the conditions for a "Canadian rap superstar" recognized in urban music's epicenter of the United States, Aubrey Graham might have never become Drake. Drake has always humbly acknowledged how these historical rap figures helped pave the way for his ultimate success and helped slay the inferiority complex most Canadian rappers have always felt living so close to the U.S.

"'Stick to Your Vision' and '416/905' were legendary moments in my life," said Drake as an endorsement on Maestro's *Stick to Your Vision* book. "Those two songs let me know that it was possible to make a city so far removed feel like it was a part of it all. Now every song and move I make I think about my people back home and how proud I am of them and they are of me. I owe a part of my confidence as a rapper to Maestro."

Canada's rap godfather Maestro seemed equally intrigued by this young rap phenomenon who is 20 years his junior. Maestro's debut, 1989's *Symphony in Effect*, was the first Canadian rap album to receive platinum certification. The emcee also did the rapper-cum-actor routine like many before him, and actually met Drake on a TV set, and not in the rap studio. "I was filming *Instant Star* and he was filming *Degrassi: The Next Generation*," explained Maestro. "I was surprised, because I only knew him as an actor; I had no idea he was an emcee/singer. I knew he had skills when I heard a few of his early songs on mixtapes but to see his career pop off like this internationally makes a brother smile."

In *Stick to Your Vision*, Maestro seemed more impressed by the fact that Drake didn't let his Canadianness slow him down or limit his dreams: "Although Drake is much younger than I am, he has inspired me because he is the ultimate example of what can happen when you Stick to Your Vision. He knew he wanted to be a recording artist, and although Canada is not exactly the home of platinum-selling hip hop record labels, he didn't let that stop him. He continued hustling, putting more mixtapes on the internet as well as doing some serious collaborations, and the rest is history."

Another Canadian rap icon who influenced Drake's early ideas around the possibility of becoming a legitimate Toronto rap super-star is Kardinal Offishall. "I remember walking through Yorkdale Mall and seeing Kardinal and being like, 'Yo, I wonder if I'll ever get a chance to say hi to that guy,'" recalled Drake. "I was on the show at the time, I was still somebody, but I remember that feeling. . . . I always wanted to do music and I was like I wonder if I'll ever get to do a track with that guy."

Despite Drake's success, Kardinal is not fully convinced a local rap revolution is taking place. "There's a buzz going on out here about Toronto, for sure, but I'm not sure if it's a movement," explained the artist now working with Bystorm Entertainment, led by Mark Pitts, the late Notorious B.I.G.'s manager. "Despite the success of Drake, K'naan, there would have to be more of a unifica-tion vibe, involving more than a couple of people, it would have to be a citywide movement. When L.A. was on the map, it was a whole movement of people working towards one goal. New York the same thing, an organic movement that has a sound it can claim. When 'Dangerous' started zooming up the charts, and when I was doing stuff with Lady Gaga, it was one person doing great things, which does not mean the whole city will now be taking stuff over. Imagine the power of myself, K'naan, Drake, if we started to throw events together, or a concert, or a party, or a charity event, or music-oriented stuff, something that means something to the community. To me, that's how you start movements."

For now, Drake's just proud to show off his hometown. His "Headlines" video pays homage to Toronto landmarks like the CN Tower and Rogers Centre, and he sports a fitted Toronto Blue Jays cap in the clip. But no matter how much he loves his hometown, like many entertainers before him, Drake faced a career ceiling in Toronto. When asked by *Peace* magazine, pre–*Thank Me Later*, where he saw himself living in the future, he seemed a bit torn largely due to the limited career prospects in his hometown. "My heart is in Toronto, and this city definitely inspires me, but I enjoy L.A. and Atlanta. . . . I'll probably get back into acting which means moving to Los Angeles." Drake eventually moved to Los Angeles in early 2012.

THE FRESH PRINCE OF FOREST HILL?

There's no reason to believe that Drake will be hanging up his microphone in the Air Canada Centre rafters anytime soon. Or that he will completely cast his rap dreams aside and pursue a full-time acting career, following in the footsteps of Will Smith, another squeaky clean platinum-selling rapper-cum-actor. When *Vibe* magazine dubbed him as "The New Fresh Prince," it might have been premature, as Smith is the only actor in history to have over eight consecutive films gross over $100 million in the domestic box office. But on the surface it's easy to see where the comparisons come from. They share similar rapper/actor trajectories, boy-next-door good looks and natural charm. Similar comparisons have been made with Childish Gambino (Donald Glover), whose debut CD was released the same day as *Take Care*, and who also boasted a strong fanbase from his acting portfolio before he was taken seriously as a rapper. Outside of LL Cool J or Ice T, there are few A-list rappers that have been able to make the successful switch from rhyme spitter to master thespian.

Academy Award–winner Jamie Foxx, who featured Drake on the remix of his "Digital Girl" single in June 2009 and in his "Fall for Your Type" video, is an interesting and rare example of an urban music star who took the opposite approach to Will Smith, shoring up his film career before pursuing his first love, music. A decorated actor, Foxx has openly admired Drake's infinite potential as a triple-threat performer, even offering up mentorship. "I'm going to be watching that young man and helping him every step of the way because I think he can really be a superstar," the acclaimed singer-actor said in an interview before a Toronto concert. Despite the many journalistic comparisons between Drake and Smith, Drake has said he derives inspiration from other actors, many without musical involvement. He's a huge fan of fellow Canadian Michael Cera as well as Evan Ross, who he told *Seventeen* he would like to play him in a biopic. He also credits Leonardo DiCaprio for influencing his career aspiration as an actor. "I like the way Leonardo DiCaprio carries himself and how much he lives his work," said Drake about the *Titanic* star. "That is something that I hope to accomplish. I don't think I live my work." Then there's his gushing over fellow Canadian teen TV drama star Ryan Gosling: the emcee told *Vibe*, "I love what he's been able to do."

But Drake cites Denzel Washington as being the one actor who made him want to pursue the craft seriously: "I remember watching the actors workshop, and Denzel Washington said that he still takes acting classes. And I was just like, 'Who's gonna teach Denzel W. how to act?'" he said. "But then I thought to myself, 'It doesn't matter who it is, it's just the fact that he's just trying to get better, and even if he sits there the whole time and learns one small thing, that makes him better.' And I feel like believing that much in my talent that I don't have to keep honing my skills is like taking it for granted almost. So I continue to try and get better."

Looking through a Hollywood prism Drake's acting career has developed slowly, with him chomping at tiny bits and bites of roles, slowly building up his IMDb profile. He had his first Hollywood role in the 2007 movie *Charlie Bartlett* with Robert Downey Jr. "It's not a huge role in the movie, but it was fun to be on that set because . . . there's a lot of names attached to it that I think we'll see a lot more of in the future," he said of his involvement in the film that was shot in Toronto's Northern Secondary School for one day. "There's a couple kids from *Degrassi* in it, a few friends of mine that I'm pretty close with," he added.

By 2009, rather than sit around and wait for roles to be offered to him, Drake started getting involved behind the scenes to develop his own content, much like many buzzy thespians on the rise have done before him. Drake signed a deal with the Toronto-based Nightingale Company in 2009 to develop a comedy series titled *Us & Them*, joining his *Degrassi: The Next Generation* colleague Mazin Elsadig. The show was to be based somewhat on the real life events of the two friends who are a contrast of each other, yet at the same time complement each other. Described as a younger version of *Entourage*, it wasn't picked up.

The one thing that has perhaps held back his actorly ambitions is that his music career is still very young. Having only released two full-length albums, Drake's hinted at how juggling the two professions might be an issue until he releases a set of legendary CDs. Music has always come first, as his talent agent explained to *Billboard*. In the lead-up to *Thank Me Later*, Drake had been reading movie scripts and turned down a number of roles.

A relative newbie in music industry and acting terms, Drake explained why he enjoys navigating the music industry over the acting industry. "The one thing that always threw me off about acting was the amount of things you have to wait for, you have to wait for so many things to fall into place before you can actually do your job," he told MuchMusic. "You gotta get the audition, you gotta have a project that's for you, you have to get the part and then the project has to get greenlit. The process of waiting to work, I don't like waiting to work."

Just as Drake is meticulous about who he gets his production beats from and who he chooses to collaborate with musically, his management team's plan of attack on the wider entertainment industry is just as cautious and selective. Drake's manager, Cortez Bryant, implied to *Vibe* magazine that he doesn't want his artist taking on stereotypical acting roles: "Drake is looking to come out with the role no one else expects. He's not gonna be the teen heart-throb or the college kid. He wants roles where he can show his acting skills. Like a sci-fi or action picture."

Organizations like the NAACP (National Association for the Advancement of Colored People) have taken up the issue of racism in Hollywood given the few non-stereotypical roles offered to black actors, and the few roles available in general. Drake told *XXL* magazine about his disappointment in the movie role choices offered up to him, the "typical projects that they'd offer to a new rapper," and hinted at the effect of race in Hollywood casting. "I want to be involved in great film projects. I don't want to do the basketball movie that everyone does," he said. "I don't want to do the typical black film that everyone expects. I think that I have enough experience to actually be involved in a real meaty project full of substance."

He almost had such a role when he was slated to play a good short role in the financial thriller *Arbitrage* written and directed by Nicholas Jarecki and featuring big names like Al Pacino and Susan Sarandon, but he didn't end up playing the role. Drake did spend some limited time back on movie sets, when he and fellow

Drake performs at the Grammys in 2012 (© Frank Micelotta/PictureGroup)

rapper Ludacris had cameo spots playing themselves in the 2011 film *Breakaway*. Directed by Robert Lieberman, *Breakaway* is an English-Punjabi comedy filmed in Toronto that tells the story of South Asian immigrants adapting to life in a new country. To date, Drake's most significant Hollywood role utilized his vocal skills. In the fourth installment of the animated Ice Age series, *Ice Age: Continental Drift*, released in July 2012, Drake joined a cast of A-list singers and actors like Jennifer Lopez, Ray Romano and Denis Leary, among others.

To date, Drake has admitted that all of these minor roles were fun, but that his dream part would be Barack Obama, a role that wouldn't be a complete stretch given that both are biracial, clean cut and have made big impacts in their own respective worlds, both flaunting larger-than-life personas while effortlessly retaining their humility. "I hope somebody makes a movie about Obama's life soon because I could play him," he told VH1 News. But there have also been rumblings that it might be Will Smith's dream role too. (Obama once remarked that Smith would be perfect for the role because he has similarly large ears.) But Drake even indicating his interest shows his confidence in his acting abilities. "That's the goal," he said. "Any time I see him on TV, I don't change the channel, I definitely pay attention and listen to the inflections of his voice. If you ask anyone who knows me, I'm pretty good at impressions. Slowly but surely, I'm not in the study mode because nobody's called me about anything, but I just pay attention so when the day comes I'm not scrambling to learn how to speak like him."

YOUNG MONEY MULTI-MILLION-AIRE

Drake alongside Mary J. Blige at the 2010 MTV Video Music Awards (© Phil McCarten/MTV/PictureGroup)

When rappers say they are popping multiple bottles of Cristal, it can come at a price, not just to the liver, but at hundreds or thousands of dollars a bottle, to the wallet too. As one of the top live touring acts in North America (The Smoking Gun leaked documents saying Drake earns $155,000 per concert and Bieber earns $300,000), Drake naturally balls out when he can by drinking expensive champagnes like Spades or Dom Pérignon, and Hennessy cognac. From flying in private planes, owning upscale condos in Miami (like the one used as a backdrop in DJ Khaled's "I'm on One" video, which features Drake), to moving to Los Angeles and living in an estimated

$9-million mansion complete with wine cellar, waterfalls, tennis courts and in-house movie theater, Drake is not your average 40-ounce rapper.

As Drake's record label name Young Money suggests, he and labelmates Lil Wayne and their peers represent a new wave of relatively young artists who are certified multimillionaires. The key word being young, in both age and in wealth accumulation. When Drake tweeted on May 30, 2012, that "the first million is the hardest," he was quickly given some perspective by billionaire T. Boone Pickens who replied that "the first billion is a helluva lot harder." On the influential 2011 *Forbes* magazine Hip Hop Cash Kings list of rap's highest earners, Drake's estimated $11 million earnings for that fiscal year tied him for 11th highest-earning hip hop artist, despite being a relative rap newbie. He was reportedly paid an enormous amount ($250,000) to perform at former President and CEO of NBC/Universal Jeff Zucker's son Andrew's bar mitzvah. His estimated 2010 salary from touring was listed at almost $4 million, based on performing 24 dates on his Light Dreams & Nightmares tour. And that was just a fraction of the earnings that Drake, who's been attached to Sprite, 2K Sports and BlackBerry campaigns among others, has commandeered over the last few years. The rumor that Universal Motown paid Drake around $2 million in 2009, at a time when the number of musicians signing bonuses and advances had shrunk, sent ripples throughout the industry.

Drake had the very clear advantage of learning from Lil Wayne. When Drake started rolling with Wayne, *Forbes* magazine estimated Lil Wayne's annual earnings at $18 million, largely based on proceeds generated from his 2008 album, *Tha Carter III*, which sold several million copies worldwide, while his nine-month bus tour grossed $42 million. Drake went from playing small clubs to immediately engaging large stadiums, largely as a by-product of his Wayne alignment. "I've never done my own full-fledged show. Prior to this, I'd probably performed maybe 10 times in my life," he revealed about his early career opportunities of tacking on to Wayne tour dates in larger venues. Drake's narrative is still highly unusual, in that before even releasing an album proper, he was already sharing management with multimillionaire hip hop icons Wayne and Kanye West, taping flashy Sprite commercials and making good money. For example, during his rise he'd already worked on Dre's highly anticipated album *Detox* (he received his first check for $10,000 dollars for "just being there," he said), and had all of the accoutrements of A-list rap living.

He had help getting there, but what has kept Drake on the lips of many influencers and rising on successive *Forbes* lists has been a series of shrewd high-stakes business moves, created to cut across industries and speak to his overall pop culture influence. For example, when LeBron James launched his *The LeBrons* family entertainment web series on YouTube in April 2011, he made sure Drake was cast in the series. (He appears as himself in one episode.) In one of his most splashy PR moves to date, Drake hung out with billionaire Richard Branson to officially celebrate the launch of Virgin America airline's California to Toronto route. Branson threw a "mile-high" style party on June 29, 2010, and named the plane *Air Drake* in an attempt to bottle up the emcee's buzz. Given that Drake's career has been orchestrated by brilliant executives like Cortez Bryant and Wayne, the launch of *Air Drake* came complete with a mention of his new album, *Thank Me Later*, which had just dropped two weeks earlier. While Richard Branson is sometimes depicted as a raging capitalist who only cares about one color, green, the charitable aspect of the new airline — Virgin Unite, which assists low-income youth in reaching their goals — is alleged to have been one of the reasons Drake had no issue co-signing another Branson brainchild.

As Drake's earning potential rose, so too did his willingness to attach himself to worthwhile humanitarian causes. Once described in *Billboard* by William Morris Agency board member

Dave Wirtschafter as being "a guy who is genuinely philanthropic . . . a guy who wants to pay real attention to people who can be benefited by his aid," Drake has ensured that as he moves forward he keeps giving back.

Outside of donating money to worthwhile causes, he did a "Stay Strapped" advertisement campaign to promote safe sex and performed with his friend Trey Songz and other rappers at an HIV/AIDS awareness concert for urban youth in November 2009 in San Bernardino, California. Drake has also in the past teamed up with former president Bill Clinton to host fundraising events for the Clinton Foundation, which encourages people under 45 to get involved in issues from climate change to economic development.

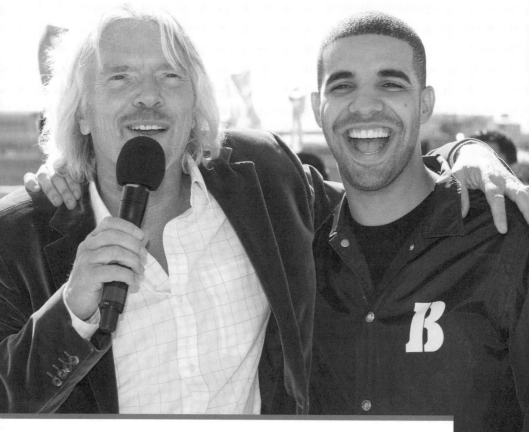

Billionaire Sir Richard Branson harnesses Drake's star power (© Robin Wong/PR Photos)

At a time when too many high-profile rappers make head-lines for all the wrong reasons, among them incarcerations, gun charges, drug addiction and dealing, very little is written about their altruism and philanthropic efforts. For example, when 50 Cent's name is mentioned in pop culture, folks tend to focus on him getting into beefs with fellow rappers like Rick Ross and sur-viving gunshot wounds. Much less ink is devoted to his pledge to provide food for one billion (yes, billion) kids in Africa by 2016, with profits from sales of his Street King energy drinks. So why is it then that these giving back gestures receive so little attention? Certainly, when Drake generously performed at the "SOS Saving Ourselves: Help for Haiti" show in Miami, Florida, on February 5, 2010, it should have showed up in those same feature stories reserved for the exploits of the Kardashians.

In his short career lifespan to date, Drake has done an equally fabulous job of giving back in different parts of the world that have touched him, including his hometown of Toronto. Drake has a foundation that works with the Sick Kids Foundation in Toronto to provide music education, and at Canada's 2011 Walk of Fame Awards gala, when he received an Allan Slaight Award for achieve-ment by a young Canadian, he donated the $10,000 honorarium that comes with the award to Dixon Hall, a community service agency that aims to create opportunities for people in low-income neighborhoods in Toronto.

Concerned with the degradation of the earth's environment, Drake has embraced the green movement. "Everywhere you turn, you can see how pollution and poverty are hurting our neigh-borhoods," he said. "But we can change that. Going green is the solution." In the lead-up to his debut *Thank Me Later*, Drake part-nered up with Green the Block and traveled to 17 campuses in 12 states to educate his fans about the benefits of going green — the jobs, health and wealth created through this movement.

Outside of North America, when it was reported that Drake

was hanging out with future Cash Money labelmate Mavado in Jamaica during the filming of his video, not nearly enough was being written about how both artists had been working together to improve the circumstances of low-income youth in Cassava Piece community in Kingston, a city with one of the highest murder rates in the world. In 2011, Drake donated $25,000 to Mavado's Gully Side charity to help build a learning center in Cassava Piece. As Mavado's manager Julian Jones-Griffith explained in Jamaica's *Weekend Star*, "Basically Mavado and Drake shot some scenes in Cassava Piece and struck up an immediate rapport with the people there. He thought they showed him a lot of love and he was very down to earth with them and wanted to do something positive." Added Drake, "Education is the key to life so to be able to assist in that process is very fulfilling."

THE DRIZZY EFFECT ON THE WEEKND

Drake in a Young Money/Cash Money Billionaires T (©PRN/PR Photos)

Mostly everything Drake touches turns into the gold that he flaunts on the cover of *Take Care*. Or rather, more than a few things he tweets or retweets trend and turn into street platinum status. Drake has unconsciously created a cottage industry, whereby many artists he collaborates with, endorses, raves about, hangs with, parties alongside or is loosely affiliated with get greenbacks and opportunities that otherwise arguably would not come their way. And their lives immediately change for the better, fiscally. And fast.

One could call it the Drizzy Effect.

Some tales of the Drizzy Effect fit in neatly in a new music world where remixes reign supreme, and where producers and artists are always looking for ways to generate quick interest in their music. His producers (T-Minus, Boi-1da and 40) are now an in-demand Hip Hop Holy Trinity. T-Minus, who got his first notable production credit on Drake's early hit "Replacement Girl," now boasts production credits on some of the finest urban hit songs of the last few years including Nicki Minaj's "Moment 4 Life" and DJ Khaled's "I'm on One." (Obscure self-taught Indian-born songwriter Nikhil Seetharam [a.k.a. Kromatik], who settled in Ajax, Ontario, after coming to Canada at a young age, also boasts credits on the aforementioned Minaj and Khaled tracks, due to his connection with T-Minus, who he met in the same suburb.)

Artist Nick Carter Green, who remixed Drake's "Headlines" in video form, was greeted with 1 million hits in the first few hours, surpassing 5.3 million views within days and achieving instant notoriety. Even Drake's Young Money labelmate Tyga's cache has certainly benefited from Drake's guest appearing on Tyga's hit singles like "Still Got It." But sometimes all it takes is a tweet. Celebrities get paid thousands of dollars for their tweets (e.g. Khloé Kardashian costs around U.S. $9,100 according to prices listed by social media marketer Izea in June 2012), but before this practice was a 140 character cash cow, Drake's pro bono endorsements helped make careers or bolstered them. One particular artist whose life got turned upside down as a result of the Drizzy Effect is starting to become an urban legend. Toronto-based visual artist Jeff Garcia's life changed forever simply because Drake liked his artwork. His story began when Drake, who is a huge fan of the late R&B starlet Aaliyah (he sports an Aaliyah tattoo on his back, honored the nine-year anniversary of Aaliyah's death in 2010 with a letter posted on RapRadar.com, sampled her vocals on "Unforgettable" and is rumored to be involved with producing her posthumous album) saw some of Garcia's work devoted to her being. "Ever since I was a kid, I've always had this crazy love for Aaliyah," Garcia told *The Grid*. "So I decided to do this tribute collage on her birthday. I was going to release it as a T-shirt around the 10th anniversary of her death."

Garcia produced a small run of his Aaliyah Kaleidoscope tribute T-shirts. When he included Drake's name in a tweet about the shirt, Drake somehow tracked Garcia down and ordered some of the artist's tees. The way he met Drake in person was right out of a Hollywood movie. It was 2 a.m., and "after expressing interest in the shirts, he sent a car to come get me. I got picked up in a Range Rover, and with all of these security guards," said the Filipino-Canadian, who is better known by his arty nom de plume Mango Peeler. "The shirts were literally just completed. I pulled the shirts off the rack — they were still drying — and he bought my first batch of 25 shirts. When they saw the shirts, they really liked them, said they loved the third world influence, and they called it 'psycho swag.'"

Clothing companies generally have to work hard to secure celebrity endorsements as a way to make their clothes seem more legit and genuine. It's a concept that was pioneered by Run-DMC in the mid-'80s when they signed the first endorsement deal between a hip hop artist and a major corporation, Adidas. The trio had already released a song of their own called "My Adidas" in 1986 that paid tribute to the shell-toed Superstar shoe they enjoyed wearing onstage. Then, before you knew it, a huge segment of hip hop humanity was wearing Adidas apparel from head to toe — and this trend continues to this day. Adidas signed an advertising deal with the group for $1 million after realizing how much promotion their product received from the trio.

In the new millennium, much of this brokering and bartering happens online. When Drake lends a ringing endorsement to a product, whether pro bono or paid, he's bringing his millions of Twitter followers along for the ride. Garcia had been exporting most of his custom-made shirts to Japan for between $75 and $250 U.S. When Drake retweeted his wares, all of a sudden the already busy artist started getting inundated with requests for his work.

Said Garcia, "He retweeted [the link], and shit went so viral. Sales were going crazy, from the U.K. to Oakland to New York." With proceeds from the influx of sales, Garcia was able to open up his own commercial art studio Halo Halo Village to teach art classes. (For the past half decade prior to that he had been traveling around Toronto teaching art.) The Drake T-shirt purchases and the orders coming in from his followers online created an immediate stimulus package that helped cover his studio's bills. "I needed to pay for my insurance, like ASAP," said Garcia. "It came as a surprise hit. So I used [the Drake cash] to pay for it. He helped pay for my insurance!" Garcia seemed even more excited at the fact that a rapper from Toronto would support artists based in his own city. "Funding local artists is huge in my books. I was opening up my new studio at the time, and the excitement around the Aaliyah shirts acted as a gateway for people to see my other works. I've done some work around town, at some cool new bars, and the Drake buzz gets mentioned. He's a tastemaker, so it helps."

While Garcia is a small business entrepreneur still riding the wave of post-Drake endorsement popularity, certainly no take on the Drizzy Effect is more intriguing than the tale of the rise of the Toronto-based Weeknd, a post-soul act who's so hot in 2012 that one woman on San Francisco's Craigslist posted that she's "willing to trade sex (1 hr)" for tickets to see him in concert. His popularity began at the end of 2010, when he got written up in the *New York Times* despite having released no official tracks online and having no album or mixtape to speak of. He didn't even have a website or a Myspace account at the time. Based on a few YouTube uploads of three songs — "What You Need," "Loft Music" and "The Morning" — *New York Times* reporter Jon Caramanica applauded the songs as a "a marvel of texture, drawing from the aching moans of screw music and the sexual impulses of early 1990s new jack swing, all buried in a hazy cloud that's part too-cool affectation, part bleeding-out puddle." He was still so underground and unknown that the esteemed publication messed up the spelling of his name. (They misspelled it as the Weekend.) At the time some folk who dubbed themselves She's So Lovely had uploaded the music and imagery most presumed was sanctioned by the Weeknd. Or was it his label? Or promotional team? No one knew.

At a time when a favorable *Pitchfork* review can make a band's career — the site is widely acknowledged as having broken other world-renowned Canadian artists like Grammy-winning Arcade Fire — it was not at all weird to read ink on an unknown upstart. What made this bizarre was that the artist had no real track record or identity to speak of and had become all the rage overnight. No one knew what the Weeknd looked like, what his government

Toronto artist Jeff Garcia benefited from a Drake retweet
(© Shiloh Bell-Higgins)

name was, who he recorded with or why. All internet sleuths had to work with were a few mentions that led back to Drizzy. In December 2010, Drake tweeted one of the lines from the Weeknd's song "Wicked Game," and the October's Very Own website featured links to the Weeknd's music. Drake then sporadically began tweeting lyrics from the Weeknd's forthcoming *House of Balloons* mixtape release.

These simple gestures only deepened the intrigue and whipped the blogosphere into a greater frenzy. Who was this mysterious psychedelic R&B artist who'd only released a few tracks? Was it Drake himself, using an alter ego to try out new material? (The production quality sounded eerily similar to the Drake sound, if there is such a thing.) Was this artist from Toronto? Memphis? Was he black or white (or both like Drake)? Who produced these hot audio treats? Was it Drake's sidekick 40? (The Weeknd eventually addressed these rumors, tweeting "40 did not produce anything on this tape . . . Shout outs to 40 though!") All music critics had to work with was that he had an affection for Michael Jackson, who he sounds like, and that he was in a past musical and production outfit called the Noise.

Almost overnight, the Weeknd now had an international audience from Toronto to Texas, page views in the six figures, and tastemakers hailing his praises as the next big thing based on a couple songs, "What You Need" and "Wicked Games," that obsessed about hard drugs, booze and popping pills aided by generic Tumblr photos largely consisting of female backsides. The songs posted online were soulful and sonically daring, and in the background were photographs of women in a hotel room. The tracks were fantastic, dark and original in a music world filled with copycats and derivative output. These songs were so original that they sounded like a genre that doesn't even really exist yet.

The response to the March 21, 2011, release of his nine-song free-for-download mixtape debut *House of Balloons* was out of this world. Nothing else out there sounded like it. Metacritic, which assigns a normalized rating based on reviews by industry professionals and fans, gave *House of Balloons* a rating of 88 indicating "Universal Acclaim," also making it the third-highest-scoring R&B release ever. Over the span of a few weeks it was downloaded more than 200,000 times.

His production team seamlessly sampled left-field numbers like Siouxsie and the Banshees' 1980 "Happy House" on "House of Balloons/Glass Table Girls" and the Cocteau Twins on "The Knowing." Some continued to believe that this Weeknd project had to be Drake's brainchild. Given his adoration of Aaliyah (his "What You Need" song begins with the same line as Aaliyah's "Rock the Boat"), the Weeknd was just Drake's sobriquet, right? In the months that followed, the mystery surrounding the Weeknd only intensified. All interview requests were declined or ignored.

But by the summer of 2011 music enthusiasts figured out that he wasn't Drake, and that this hipster R&B–leaning music was being sung by Vancouver-bred, Toronto-based Ethiopian singer/songwriter Abel Tesfaye. Listeners also deduced his age from "Loft Music," in which he seduces an unnamed female and mentions that he's only 20. For those who dug around on the web to research who was creating these wildly exciting soundscapes, the names of producers "Doc" Martin McKinney and Illangelo popped up. It was now clear that these otherworldly sounds could have only been spearheaded by rising beatsmith Illangelo and by Doc, the mastermind behind Esthero's ethereal sounds and Res's undefinable genreless music output and who had worked with Santigold. Doc had been posting mysterious Twitter feeds about the Weeknd from the beginning.

According to conventional wisdom, the Weeknd should have turned this cachet into fast cash, signing a quickie record deal from one of his many suitors and perhaps hooking up with a major promoter for a tour that would generate good gate receipts for all involved. But rather than do all of that, the Weeknd team announced their own 12th hour headlining all-ages concert at the 600-capacity Mod Club for July 24. The concert info was released only a little over a week before the date, and prospective attendees could only get tickets at a hip hoppy shoe store in downtown Toronto called Stussy. The Weeknd's team put in place a "no guest list, no cameras, no media" clause on the promotional materials, with the "no cameras" piece being quite impossible to administer or police in an age where at most concerts smartphones wave like lighters at Woodstock. The $20 concert tickets sold out within four hours. Scalpers outside the venue were asking for $200.

    This concert was Tesfaye's coming-out party, the first time

The Weeknd's first ever concert at Toronto's Mod Club (© Jason Richards)

the general public got a glimpse of who the Weeknd was. And it was surreal for all involved. Rumors of Diddy being at the show were confirmed by bloggers and fellow musicians like Massari. Drake was spotted perched up on the venue's balcony, looking on like a proud father. Members of what was later revealed to be the Weeknd's XO Crew (identifiable on Twitter by their handles, which all end in XO) were spotted in and around the venue. When Tesfaye finally emerged sporting a scruffy high-top afro and an army fatigue jacket, the audience lost their minds applauding. The most interesting observation made by many who attended was that his built-in web fanbase sounded like one nation under a groove, singing along to all nine songs word for word until the curtains came up. Tesfaye looked both nervous and composed all at the same time.

The Drake connections were immediately obvious. Adrian Eccleston, a guitarist in Drake's live touring band, was up onstage, directing the stage sounds. And on July 24 Drake tweeted, "I am so fuckin proud. You performed magic tonight." A mere week later on July 31, 2011, the Weeknd was a support act at Drake's second annual OVO Festival. While he didn't make much of an impression there — it's hard to stand out when the concert's support acts are luminaries Lil Wayne, Stevie Wonder and Nas — his legend was already being secured, and the buzz surrounding his next mixtape had grown tenfold. When the second of a trilogy of mixtapes, *Thursday*, was released on Thursday (naturally), August 17, it was downloaded an astounding 180,000 times on its first day, crashing his website. The Weeknd was forced to re-release it, using more stable file-sharing means. While some wondered whether the thinking behind issuing a third free mixtape, *Echoes of Silence*, while still not conducting any interviews and giving just a handful of live appearances, was getting a bit redundant, it might've even enhanced his position. A few hours after the release of *Echoes*, one of the top trending topics on Twitter in America was the Weeknd.

By year's end, he had landed in the top 20 of the most significant best of 2011 lists, including those of *Pitchfork, Spin* and MTV. By early January 2012, the Weeknd got booked to play his American debut and first significant large-scale live concert at Coachella, one of the most popular music festivals in the world. To prep for the gig, an audition alert was posted to his Facebook page, advertising that he was "looking for a professional guitarist and bass player in or around the Toronto area to travel and perform live in concert" with a January 8, 2012, deadline date. Given near-top billing at Coachella — he was slotted in as a third tier billing, only a few slots below Dr. Dre and Snoop Dogg and their surprise Tupac hologram — he performed songs from his three mixtapes, plus a verse from his extraordinary collaboration with Drake, "Crew Love." The widely streamed set cemented his position as a trailblazer set to redefine modern music as we know it.

By Spring 2012, just as journalists remained stymied by their attempts to get any interviews with the Weeknd, a flurry of interesting details emerged about his history from a Halifax-born, Toronto-based producer named Jeremy "Zodiac" Rose, whose name had been circulating as a possible producer since the beginning. He made public claims to being the person who gave the Weeknd his name and helped craft his sound. "I met Abel through some common friends back in 2010. Franky Gross, Ari Neville and Yoav Lester," he said in an email interview. "We were working together on the project for a month or two before we settled on a name. It was becoming the time to release some tracks so we needed something quick. We were all hanging out at Abel's place drinking beer when I came up with 'The Weekend' in accordance with the aesthetic that we were trying to convey. Everyone in the room seemed to like it so it stuck." Rose told *Vice* magazine that his uncredited production was featured on "Loft Music," "What You Need" and the original version of "The Morning" that blew the Weeknd up and that he was a part of the original group, then titled

The Weekend, with an "e." (He said of the group's demise, "Well, I left. He dropped the 'e.'") The pair split up over what were creative differences according to his interview with *Now* magazine. "At the time, he was really pushing to have more club tracks, and I wasn't feeling that," explained Rose. "He didn't really care what I thought, but I was being stubborn too." Probably the most interesting revelation made by Rose here was that he suspects the whole idea of the Weeknd not doing any interviews with media has more to do with him being "just a goofy kid, really — a bit weird" rather than being the product of some marketing savvy and masterful publicity manipulation.

Regardless of his strategy, there's no doubt that the Weeknd is indebted to Drake's paradigm-shifting example and his Midas touch. As for Drake, playing the modern-day godfather to Toronto urban music was a way to give back to his city and do what others like Wayne had done for him. But it also gives him an automatic connection to hot new hometown acts and expands the borders of the Drake Nation just a little bit further.

TAKE
CARE

The Weeknd's sonically adventurous strain of futuristic soul, abetted by Drake, created this overwhelming demand for more music from the OVOXO crew, while *Thank Me Later*'s success certainly proved that Drake could more than hold his own as both a fierce emcee and a soulful singer. He had been wanting to cement his reputation as a capable singer/songwriter for quite some time now, and what better way to prove he could compete with the R&B and soul vocal talents of the day than by releasing a straight R&B mixtape. The plan was for Drake to release the mixtape tentatively titled *It's Never Enough* to showcase his crooner side.

But he was no longer a free-wheelin' independent artist, instead he was a bit more beholden to music industry conventions and his main priority had to be the follow up to *Thank Me Later*. He took to his OVO blog on February 7, 2011, to post his feelings about his change in plans. He wrote, "I wake up and never know what to expect from any given day but good or bad I always learn something from it. I have decided that I am going to push *It's Never Enough* and focus completely on delivering *Take Care* to you all. I feel like my mind is truly ready to make this next album NOW and I don't want that feeling to escape me." *Take Care* was slated to be released on his birthday, October 24, 2011, the perfect brand-conscious choice.

To keep his fans' appetites whetted until his sophomore release came, Drake leaked the occasional single and showed up on other artists' remixes like he had done in the past. Regular followers of his October's Very Own blog were treated to some of his best music yet, from solo hardcore hip hop bangers like "Dreams Money Can Buy," to superb guest verses on SBTRKT's "Wildfire" with Little Dragon, all the way to more spacey downtempo soul numbers like "Trust Issues." Perhaps his most intriguing solo song leak, accompanied by a video, was a near six-minute slow synthesizer-fueled song titled "Marvins Room" released in June 2011. In the video Drake plays a rapper drunk on fame among other things. As artistically captivating a statement as he'd made since *So Far Gone*'s "Find Your Love," on the track Drake makes an inebriated call to a soon-to-be ex, sharing open, honest admissions. The video immediately went viral, and all of a sudden a slew of artists were remixing it. Billboard Music Award–nominated singer JoJo recorded a "Can't Do Better" remix version that gave the female protagonist in the song a voice. Teyana Taylor, a singer with rumored romantic ties to Drake, recorded another female response record, titled "Her Room." The buzz was so big on "Marvins Room" that even American Music Award–winning R&B star Chris Brown took a crack at remixing it. For those looking for Drake's new sonic direction, another leaked track, "Free Spirit," guested by Rick Ross, surfaced. Despite the positive public response to these leaked tracks, Drake's tweets revealed that he was disappointed at the response of Universal, his label's parent company, which allegedly asked that the leaked songs be taken down from sites that re-posted the songs, as well as from his own blog. He tweeted, "Universal needs to stop taking my fucking songs down. I am doing this for the people not for your label." When he offered up tweets like "Free up da man dem from captivity," it was a reminder that the pressure to appease record company interests were real, and that selflessly releasing free music for his fans to hear might be more of an issue now.

Despite these minor distractions, Drake used his media opportunities to announce that *Take Care* would showcase his musical maturity and would be his first fully genuine artistic statement to the world. *Thank Me Later* marked a time in Drake's life where he had to prove every ounce of the hype foisted on him. It was the disc he had to make. *Take Care* — whose name he came up with while on tour with Jay-Z in Europe — was the disc he always wanted to make. Of his first album he told *Rolling Stone*, "In no way am I not proud of it. I think I got caught up in making it seem big and first album–ish. I was a bit numb, a bit disconnected from myself. I wasn't able to slow down and realize what was going on around me." He approached *Take Care* differently, explaining, "The whole process has been about slowing life down and really pinpointing emotions." He told *XXL* magazine, "*Take Care* is going to be my best sonic work to date. I think that musically I'll be able to take it to another level now."

When word got out that Stevie Wonder was going to appear on the disc, it was clear he was dead serious about raising the bar. Drake told MuchMusic that working with Stevie Wonder was a dream come true. "He helped me out with a lot of the music . . . told me where I could add a couple things to make it more sonically appealing, and not only that but we actually are writing together, which is an incredible experience." Another one of his other music heroes, Andre 3000, who had declined to participate on his debut, also agreed to appear on *Take Care* ("The Real Her"). To top it all off, with the release of "Headlines," Drake had tied Diddy's *Billboard* record for most number one songs (10) on *Billboard*'s Rap Songs chart. (He has since smashed that record, with 12 number one singles, and counting.)

As Drake's birthday release date neared, his camp had reportedly still not cleared all of the samples for *Take Care* or fully mastered the disc. Having been hit by a lawsuit before for including uncleared samples from the 1975 Hamilton, Joe Frank and Reynolds ballad "Fallin' in Love," on previous hits like "Best I Ever Had," Drake's camp was not interested in going down that route again — especially given hip hop's history of lawsuits for uncleared samples, namely landmark cases involving Biz Markie and De La Soul.

Once again, Drake used his OVO blog to explain why he'd have to delay the disc's release. Whereas old-school artists might've hidden behind press releases and publicists, Drake spoke to his constituents directly. On October 8, 2011, he wrote, "The new date for *Take Care* is November 15, 2011. I managed to create this album in my hometown of Toronto. . . . This music means too much to me to get attached to dates and I do apologize for the delay but I promise that it is only for the benefit of our experience together." With this delay, the music world gave a collective sigh. Many questions remained. Was he buckling under the pressure to outdo his illustrious debut? Did he fear the dreaded sophomore jinx? Or was he having second thoughts about how he wanted to be perceived in the music industry?

None of the above held true. And these hiccups did little to slow down the Drake train. The following week, he hit the road, debuting new music in New York on Funkmaster Flex's Hot 97 radio show. He then made his *Saturday Night Live* debut performing a few comedy sketches and two cuts from the disc, "Make Me Proud" (with labelmate Nicki Minaj) and "Headlines." At a time when album leaks in the music industry have almost become a part of some hacker-devised marketing scheme that is accepted, an unauthorized leak unleashed *Take Care* a week prior to its commercial release. Drake, who was used to giving music away for free, took it all in stride (his Twitter post read, "listen, enjoy it, buy it if you like it") and he said he actually felt lucky that it wasn't leaked earlier.

At 4 a.m. the day before *Take Care's* release, his hometown fans began lining up over 12 hours before Drake was to appear at a Queen West HMV record store. Four multicultural Toronto area youth, including Deja, a 16-year-old African-Canadian teen, and her two Filipino friends, Marc and Kyle, both 15 years old, were

Drake performs on Valentine's Day 2012 at the University of Miami
(© Courtney Engelke)

anxious to get downtown from the suburbs to snag wristbands as part of a Universal Canada promotion that allowed the first 500 people to preorder *Take Care* to meet their idol. They performed this early morning feat on a school day (one of the kids' dads ushered them back and forth between school and the retailer to get the wristbands, then returned later to line up). This was hardly the most extreme story of Drake Nation devotion: a woman in Los Angeles got his name tattooed on her forehead at L.A.'s Will Rise Tattoo, perhaps taking the lyrics of "Free Spirit" to heart.

Deja and company weren't even close to being the first ones there. There were over 230 people in front of them. They had come in from as far as Edmonton, Windsor, Bermuda, Montreal and New Jersey for this event. It was a near-torrential downpour, but that didn't matter. They were here to catch a glimpse of their hero. By 4:30 p.m., a full hour before Drake was to make a grand entrance in a black SUV, with buckets of rain pouring down on everyone in the line waiting to meet him, Deja's crew of friends were feeling drunk with anticipation.

The disc was to be released the following day, November 15 (in fact, all of his CDs have been released on the 15th day of the month), so they could have waited until then to get it. But when asked why they would wake up at these ungodly hours to line up for a glimpse of Drake, Deja replied, "He's the love of my life." Another friend, Nicollette, looked on and regaled the group with tales of how Deja fell on the ground and almost got trampled while jockeying for position in line, as a group of mostly female black and South Asian teenage girls and 20-somethings sang "Marvins Room" in the rain. Of the dedicated fans, Drake said, "People slept in the rain, people came in soaked, voices gone, sick . . . all just for a 10 second interaction, that's why I stayed there for like, six, seven hours . . . when they told me don't take any pictures, and sign one thing per person, I signed six things, I had conversations with people."

A few days later Drake told MuchMusic VJ T-RexXx that he

was humbled by all of this activity, and as a gesture of good faith consciously waited to sign each and every last CD that his fans preordered that day — not the normal course of action for a mega-star of his magnitude. As the police presence and security detail around the event grew, the word on the street was that no one quite anticipated that there would be such large crowds like this, in the hundreds, standing in the rain, jamming up the street corner with this much intensity.

No one saw it coming, just like Drake himself.

On the cover of *Take Care*, a bearded semi-afroed Drake looks like a tortured artist. Surrounded by jewelry, gold cups and gold-encrusted tchotchkes, this opulent image of him makes as profound a statement as the music itself. Drake comes off as a new rap aristo-crat mulling over his money, power and respect. It also marks one of the first times that he appears comfortable with his fame — a good thing, because he was on the rise. *Take Care* debuted on the *Billboard* 200 charts at number one, selling a staggering 631,000 copies in first-week sales, 180,000 units more than his debut. *Take Care*'s success was just another career highlight, another crescendo in a long line of shining moments. For the most part, critics were as enthusiastic as fans. *Pitchfork* said *Take Care's* quality proved that "it's increasingly apparent that Drake is the most engaging new rap star since Ye" and the *New York Times* noted, "That *Take Care* is an almost complete success is no small feat, especially given that it's an accomplishment of form more than of content, content having been handled assuredly on the last two Drake releases." The *Village Voice* alt-weekly dubbed *Take Care* "as good a rap album as 2011 has had" in part because of Drake's "understanding of melody, and his willingness to sound a little more sing-songy than most rappers to make a bar more indelible." The A.V. Club called it an "immersive headphone masterwork that's tender and intimate like little else in contemporary rap and R&B."

Drake teamed up with the Weeknd on two of the most dense

cuts on the disc. In "Crew Love," a track which even gained the attention of Facebook CEO Mark Zuckerberg (he sent the Rap Genius website fan mail about the song), Drake explains, in brilliant rhyme form, his decision to serve his family and those closest to him, spiritually and fiscally. A number of the tracks sound like a futuristic bastard child of southern rap, soul, slow jam R&B, techno and sometimes trip hop. It is the epitome of the iPod generation: this was music of no nation, no genre, defying borders and easy categorization. He had created his own sound, as singular as the man himself. It's what Sugar Hill Gang's Wonder Mike appreciates the most, coming from a time in '80s hip hop when creating a distinct identity and sound mattered more than anything else. "I like people that take chances, that don't follow, Drake seems to be somewhat of a leader. He's not dictated to, hanging on to every word of the status quo. He's one of those hip hop guys that's thinking for themselves, and that's hip hop."

"Lord Knows" set the stage for many fruitful collaborations with rappers he adores, like Rick Ross. "You could sit around Rick Ross for 20 minutes, and get so many gems . . . you could understand why he's such a great rapper, because he's such a great talker," Drake told MuchMusic. On arguably the most poignant song on the disc "Look What You've Done," an open letter to his mom, uncle and *bubbe* (who appears in a voicemail), you get to witness Drake at his finest. He's heartfelt and honest in his collaboration with Canadian expat Chilly Gonzales, a one-time doubter.

Drake's musical view of the future this time around involved paying homage to the past. Thoughtfully aware of rap's history, Drake retrofitted Juvenile's 1999 hit "Back That Azz Up" into an R&B ballad for "Practice." Juvenile told *XXL* that he was touched by the gesture. "I'm kind of flattered that it was Drake and that it's an R&B song. I never pictured it to be used that way, but he did a great job with it, man."

To the curious onlooker, Drake's sales numbers, critical respect, cult-like fanbases and accolades suggest that he is one of the few icons of the contemporary music industry who might be universally shared and collectively adored. His relentless 2012 Club Paradise tour, which had him recording songs for his third CD in his tour bus studio, had a 60-plus date schedule that has kept him on the road from February to June with an assortment of acts including ASAP Rocky, Kendrick Lamar, J. Cole, Waka Flocka Flame and 2 Chainz, has kept his brand on the lips of hip hoppers, hipsters, influencers and most importantly his Drake Nation of fans who follow his every tweet religiously. But that certainly doesn't mean that everyone is drinking the Drake Kool-Aid, and that his artistic integrity hasn't and won't be vigorously challenged by some of the music industry's stalwarts.

For example, in early 2012, in what was one of the most confusing and improbable rap duels, respected Chicago-bred rap wordsmith Common dissed Drake, calling him "soft" on his single "Sweet" and referred to him as "Canada Dry" on a remix of Rick Ross's "Stay Schemin'." Given that Common is a highly respected repeat Grammy winner and one of the most feared battle rappers (his 1996 "The Bitch in Yoo" diss track aimed at fellow rapper Ice Cube is considered one of the most stylistically sound yet vicious diss raps of all time), it's a reminder that Drake's path to the ultimate rap glory won't always be paved with gold. A challenge of a different sort emerged from his alleged ex Ericka Lee, who reportedly filed a lawsuit against Drake in early 2012 claiming creative input and unpaid royalties for work on "Marvins Room."

"Why Is Drake So Angry?" asked a cover blurb on the February 2012 issue of *Vibe* magazine. The feature story by Lola Ogunnaike titled "The Dark Side of Aubrey Graham" lays out the possibility that Drake's innocence, spurred on by his liberal Canadian upbringing, might be more diminished as he becomes a full-on mega celebrity. This portrait of Drake expressed some fears from the rap cognoscenti that he might be morphing into a prima

donna, the exact opposite of the modest kid from safe, conservative Toronto he started out as. The story gives an example, a tantrum he threw when he saw that the magazine's stylists didn't carry clothes he wanted to wear for the cover story photo shoot — a shoot he allegedly arrived for more than eight hours late. The American rap culture is rough on its own, and in the spread Miss Info asks more tough questions, chipping away at his integrity. "Why is he trying to look thugged out? Why does he have a Southern Drawl when he's from Canada?" While to some, beef is only cow's meat, in hip hop it's a rite of passage, so emcees like Drake gunning for the top spot have to be ready.

In the wider court of public opinion, certainly Drake's appeal to teens, tweens, baby boomers, those both black and white like his racial composition, and everyone in between, speaks to the coming of a new day in music, in society, where hopefully one's race might matter less. Post-racial poster boy? Perhaps.

What will be Drake's lasting legacy, once he decides to hang up the mic in the rafters? It's far too early to tell. Some, like rapper Promise, foresaw that Drake had what the late Miles Davis might call "that thing," that essential but indefinable quality that makes one rise above the rest. But even Promise marvels at how far he has come. "I had no idea he was gonna blow up like how he did, at the speed or level, but I knew he'd be something big someday."

However, what is certain is that he wants to be considered one of the greatest wordsmiths of our time, someone who crafted great rhymes, as most legendary emcees should, lines that future legions of rappers can study and pass on for generations. "I think one of my biggest things is to be quoted," he told *Metro*. "I grew up reading quotes, studying what intelligent people had to say, what wise people had to say, so I think one of my biggest goals in life is just to be a quoted individual, and to be somebody whose words matter."

Drake is a great role model for youth who have ever felt insignificant but deep down inside knew they had something important to contribute to society, to art, to culture. As Drake told MuchMusic, "I was never popular, I wasn't a popular kid. I wasn't cool. I'm cool now though, things change. So I just really wanna be something positive for this generation, that's all."

If there's one thing that's clear, it's that Drake's success represents a new day. A new day for the myriad of historically black musics, from hip hop to R&B to soul to electronic, that show up in his sonic mix can to be heard together. A far cry from the time when R&B/funk outfit Crack of Dawn became the first Toronto-based black music act to sign to a major label recording contract in 1974. Trevor Daley, the band's trombone player, believes that Drake's success is a natural by-product of decades of struggle to have certain musics heard more widely. "He represents us well as black people, as Canadians, and I'm glad that he's doing it with class," said Daley. His band only got around $50,000 as an advance to get their 1975 debut album done and had to rely on money made from playing live gigs — they played weekly weekend gigs averaging about $3,000–5,000 a week in earnings over a two- to three-year period — demonstrating the more things change, the more they stay the same.

Unlike Drake, most musicians of today have to solely rely on tour earnings to sustain themselves. "In a certain sense right now, it gives me a feeling of pride, maybe we did in some way open some doors, so other people can come through it. There's no direct correlation between our breakthrough and his success, but it makes us feel good," said Daley. Alvin Jones, the band's saxophone and flute player, still can't believe a Toronto kid could break through like this. "I just wonder how did he do that? How he was able to break through to that music royalty with Jay-Z. I couldn't believe it's the same kid from *Degrassi*."

On "Lord Knows" Drake seems to have some idea of where he hopes to be, stature-wise, rhyming off the names of Bob Marley and Jimi Hendrix, whose *Live at Woodstock* DVD he'd carried on his tour bus in the past as a lucky charm. For someone who once told a *GQ* reporter, "I'm obsessed with perfection," it may not be such a far stretch for him to dream that big. And despite the heavy influence of his birthplace Toronto on his music, life and loves, now that he's based in the City of Angels, no one knows what a newer, more seasoned Drake will offer up to the world. While addressing his relocation to L.A., Drake remarked to *Billboard*, "There's a new atmosphere. I'm getting to know new people. . . . Anybody knows that when it's new, that's when I thrive. When there's new things to talk about that's really when I get off." Clearly, Drake's time on the world stage and his artistic contributions are far from over.

Selected Sources

1loveTO.com.

Ahearn, Victoria. "Drake's Young Writer-friends Were Behind Juno
Skits," The Canadian Press. March 31, 2011.

Allen III, Roosevelt. "Hip Hop Artist Pays Homage to Drake and
Yields Over 5 Million Views," Metro Media Consulting Group.
October 7, 2011.

Allthings-fresh.net (site discontinued).

Arceneaux, Michael. "Drake Becomes Latest Victim of Concert
Scam," BET.com. April 6, 2011.

———. "Rihanna Denies Dating Drake," BET.com. June 16, 2011.

"Aubrey Drake Graham Interview." NotableInterviews.com.

December 11, 2007. http://www.notableinterviews.com/
aubrey-drake-graham-interview/.

Barshad, Amos. "Drake: The Heeb Interview," HeebMagazine.com.
June 18, 2010.

Beckford, Mark. "Video with Movado Bad for Jamaica?" *Jamaica Gleaner.* May 12, 2010.

BMI Songwriter of the Year Awards. August 27, 2011. http://www
.rap-up.com/2011/08/27/drake-accepts-bmi-songwriter-of-the-
year-award-video/.

Boles, Benjamin. "JUNO Award April Fools?" *Now.* April 2, 2012.

———. "Ex-Member of the Weeknd Comes Out of Hiding," *Now.*
March 22, 2012.

Bradley, Adam, and Andrew DuBois. *The Anthology of Rap.* New
Haven/London: Yale University Press, 2010.

Brennan, Morgan. "Rapper Drake Finds an A-List Home Buyer in
Under 24 Hours," Forbes.com. March 12, 2012.

Brown, Darius. ABC News interview. July 15, 2009. http://www
.youtube.com/watch?v=3njbUN2RG4s.

Caramanica, Jon. "The New Face of Hip Hop," *New York Times.*
June 9, 2010.

———. "Drake Pushes Rap Toward the Gothic," *New York Times.*
November 16, 2011.

Chung, Alexa. *It's On with Alexa Chung.* Aired February 2010.
http://www.youtube.com/watch?v=KTc_OlMgUQk.

CNN Interview. "Rapper Makes Ladies Toss Undergarments."
Aired May 4, 2010. http://www.cnn.com/video/#/video/
showbiz/2010/05/04/nat.drake.interview.cnn.

Concepcion, Mariel. "Drake: The Billboard Cover Story," *Billboard.*
May 21, 2010.

Creekmur, Chuck. "Top 5 Dead or Alive: Drake," AllHipHop.com.
July 8, 2010.

Crosley, Hilary. "Sade on Drake Collabo: Thanks but No Thanks," MTV.com. February 16, 2010.

Cummings, Jozen. "Dream Date: At long last, hip-hop wunderkind Drake has arrived," *Paper.* June 18, 2010.

"Deconstructing Drake," ASCAP Music Expo, Los Angeles. April 29, 2011. http://www.youtube.com/watch?v=PDZdqWlStw8.

Degrassi-fans.com.

Degrassi Unscripted: Aubrey Graham (Jimmy). Epitome Pictures. 2004.

De la Cruz, Noelia. "Drake Admits to Sweater Obsession," Vulture.com. September 9, 2011.

Deziel, Shanda. "Drake Superior," Macleans.ca. June 22, 2009.

Digital, Rez, and Ty Harper. Drake interview. *OTA Live*, Flow 93.5 FM. May 11, 2007. http://www.youtube.com/watch?v=XlrbCozQn-A.

Doucette, Chris. "Toronto man wanted for defrauding hip hop artists," *Toronto Sun.* May 19, 2011.

DrakeDaily.com.

DrakeNews.com.

DrakeOfficial.com.

Drake-Online.com.

"Drake Slams Universal for Taking New Songs Off the Internet," Billboard.com. June 24, 2011.

DrizzyDrake.org.

Facebook.com/theweeknd.

Fennessey, Sean. "Backstory: Noah '40' Shebib," GQ.com. November 10, 2011.

Ferdinand, Rio. Interview with Drake, 5mag.com. http://www.youtube.com/watch?v=jQT38g1XL2M.

Frushtick, Russ. "Drake to Star in 'Gears of War 3,'" MTV.com. June 11, 2010.

Garraud, Tracy. "Stop Comparing Kardinal Offishall to Drake," Vibe.com. April 6, 2010.

Gissen, Jesse. "Boi-1da: A Star Is Born," XXLmag.com. September 11, 2009.

Graff, Gary. "Drake Was 'Down' on 'Take Care,' Says Third Album Will Be Different," Billboard.com. April 24, 2012.

Green, Mark Anthony. "The GQ & A: Drake," *GQ*. November 11, 2011.

Greenburg, Zack O' Malley. "Cash Kings 2011: Hip-Hop's Top Earners," Forbes.com. August 9, 2011.

———. "Hip-Hop's Cash Kings 2010," Forbes.com. August 17, 2010.

Gupta, Sanjay. "Following MS Diagnosis, The Beat Goes On," CNN. April 17, 2012. http://thechart.blogs.cnn.com/2012/04/17/the-beat-goes-on-for-music-producer-diagnosed-with-multiple-sclerosis/?iref=allsearch.

Handler, Chelsea. Interview with Drake, *Chelsea Lately*. Aired November 22, 2011. http://www.youtube.com/watch?v=FnF_asQnAa0.

Hines, Horace. "Police Pull Plug on Drake," *Jamaica Observer*. March 16, 2011.

Hoffman, Claire. "On the Cover: Drake," *GQ*. April 2012.

"'Hollaback' T. Slack: The Midas Touch of Music," TheIndustrySpotlight.blogspot.ca. November 11, 2009.

Houghton, Edwin. "Drake's Rise to Fame and Fortune," TheFader.com. September 1, 2009.

Hustlegrl.com.

Industry. June 2009. http://www.industry-mag.com/jun09.pdf (site discontinued).

Infantry, Ashante. "Chasing Drake," *Toronto Star*. June 21, 2009.

Itzkoff, Dave. "Drake Concert Is Canceled at Seaport," *New York Times*. June 15, 2010.

Jacobs, Justin. "Page Explains Beef with Drake: 'He's a Snitch and a Coward,'" TheBoombox.com. April 7, 2010.

Jones, Jen. "School's in for Degrassi," Jvibe.com. December 2006. http://www.jvibe.com/Pop_culture/Degrassi.php.

Jordan, Harrison. "Degrassi Actor Says Being Different Made Him Stronger," *Canadian Jewish News*. December 21, 2006.

Juice DVD Volume II: The All-Stars. Brothers Entertainment, 2006.

Kaplan, Ben. "Enter Canada: Wu-Tang Clan Come North of the Border," *National Post*. November 28, 2011.

Kaufman, Gil. "Drake Reveals Next Album to Be Called Take Care," MTV.com. November 17, 2010.

Kimmel, Jimmy. "Tweet Tweet" sketch, *Jimmy Kimmel Live*. Aired June 24, 2010. http://www.youtube.com/watch?v=vr8DyYLT4DE.

Langhorne, Cyrus. "Sade on Not Collaborating w/ Kanye West & Drake, 'I've Always Avoided Working Outside My Safety Zone,'" SOHH.com. February 16, 2010.

La Puma, Joe. "Justin Bieber Talks Drake Collaboration and More," Complex.com. April 9, 2010.

Leblanc, Larry. "In the Hot Seat with Larry Leblanc — Industry Profile: Cortez Bryant," CelebrityAccess.com. December 6, 2010.

Lester, Paul. "Drake: 'Why Do You Hate Me So Much?,'" *Guardian*. March 29, 2012.

Liss, Sarah. "Next Stop, Wonderland," *Grid*. March 21, 2012.

Mancini, Elam, and Benjamin Meadows-Ingram. "Drake Disappointed with Movie Offers," *XXL*. May 2010.

Maness, Carter. "How Bad Do You Want It," *XXL*. June 2011.

Markman, Rob, and Sway Calloway. "Drake Has a 'Good' Feeling About Justin Bieber Collabo," MTV.com. May 23, 2012.

Martinez, Angie. *The Angie Martinez Show*, Hot 97 FM. April 16, 2009. http://www.youtube.com/watch?v=CRBE4BNKHkc&playnext=1&list=PLO23D6361EEAC80B7.

———. *The Angie Martinez Show*, Hot 97 FM. October 5, 2010.

McGuire, Patrick. "How the Producer of The Weeknd's Breakout Tracks Got Majorly Screwed," Vice.com. March 22, 2012.

McKinnon, Matthew. "Almost Famous," *Walrus*. May 2010.

Meadows-Ingram, Benjamin. "Drake Leaves ICM But Stays with Hip Hop Since 1978, Contrary to Reports," Billboard.biz. December 1, 2011.

———. "Drake: William Morris' Dave Wirtschafter Talks About Agency's Big Plans for the Superstar MC-Actor," Billboard.biz. November 11, 2011.

———. "Drake: The Billboard Q&A," Billboard.com. November 11, 2011.

Mindbender. "Utterly Disrespectful" (audio and transcribed lyrics). http://mindbendersupreme.bandcamp.com/track/utterly-disrespectful.

Mistry, Anupa. "A D-sisive Issue," TorontoStandard.com. November 16, 2011.

Monet, Lissa. "Drake Enters The Centre," *Peace*. Issue #94, 2009.

MTV. *Drake: Better Than Good Enough*. TV special. Aired June 23, 2010.

MTV. *When I Was 17* (Ep. 3 Drake, Jennie Finch, Queen Latifah). TV special. Aired May 15, 2010.

MuchMusic interview. "Drake: The Homecoming." Aired November 14, 2011. http://www.muchmusic.com/tv/specials/drakethehomecoming/cid/569208/-drake-interview.

MuchMusic. *Born To Be: Drake*. November 2009.

Myspace.com/thisisdrake.

Narduwar. "Narduwar vs. Drake interview." http://nardwuar.com/vs/drake/.

OctobersVeryOwn.net.

Ogunnaike, Lola. "The Dark Side of Aubrey Graham," *Vibe*. March 2012.

———. "Everybody Loves Drake," *Vibe*. December 2009.

Ostroff, Joshua. "Aubrey Graham: from Degrassi to Drake," *Globe and Mail*. March 23, 2009.

———. "Juno Awards 2012: Drake Loses Best Album to Michael

Buble 'Christmas' Album, Feist Wins Best Artist," Spinner.ca.
April 1, 2012.

"Page and Drake Beef Comes Out in the Open!," Life Pulse
Blog. March 26, 2010. http://lifepulseblog.com/2010/03/26/
page-and-drake-beef-comes-out-in-the-open/.

Patch, Nick. "Kardinal Offishall: Junos disrespected Drake," The
Canadian Press. May 6, 2011.

Phillips, Jerica. "Dad Describes Years Hip Hop Star Drake Spent in
Memphis," WMCTV.com. November 14, 2011.

Plambeck, Joseph. "Playboy Sues Drake for Copyright
Infringement," *New York Times*. June 29, 2010.

RapGenius.com.

"Red Hot Vocal Coach for Usher, Keri Hilson, Trey Songz and
Justin Bieber Snags Another High Profile Client, DRAKE," *All
Radio News*. April 2010. http://www.jansmith.com/2010/04/
red-hot-vocal-coach-for-usher-keri-hilson-trey-songz-and-
justin-bieber-snags-another-high-profile-client-drake.

Reid, Shaheem. "Nicki Minaj Calls Drake Twitter Marriage
'Mischievous,'" MTV.com. September 7, 2010.

————. "Drake Signs with Lil Wayne's Young Money Label," MTV.com.
June 29, 2009.

————. "Drake's So Far Gone Is the Hottest Mixtape of 2009 (So
Far)," MTV.com. July 16, 2009.

———— and Matt Elias. "Drake Still Hopeful for a Collaboration
with Sade 'One Day,'" MTV.com. March 18, 2010.

———— and Sway Calloway. "Exclusive: Drake's Thank Me Later
Due June 15," MTV.com. April 5, 2010.

Richards, Jason. "Gonzales Thanks Drake Later," NowToronto.com.
March 30, 2011.

————. "Boi-1da," *Now*. March 24, 2011.

Richburg, Chris. "Drake Plans New Lawsuit Over Unauthorized
New Album," AllHipHop.com. June 7, 2009.

Rodriguez, Jayson. "Drake Calls 'Light Up,' His Collabo with Jay-Z, 'Phenomenal,'" MTV.com. December 30, 2009.

———. "Drake Apologizes to Head of Motown for Slam," MTV.com. August 13, 2009.

Rosenberg, Peter. Interview, Rosenberg Radio. May 27, 2009.

Saltsman, Peter. "Reasons to Love Toronto Now: Because Drake Had Babies," *Toronto Life*. June 2012.

Scaggs, Austin. "Drake on Visiting Hendrix's Grave, His Motivational Tweets and His Trips to See Lil Wayne in Prison," *Rolling Stone*. September 30, 2010.

SceneandHeard.ca.

Shallcross, Juliana. "Virgin America's 'Air Drake' Lands in Toronto, with Richard Branson and Arnold Schwarzenegger in Tow," Jaunted.com. June 30, 2010.

Smooth, Jay. "Mark Drake's Words," VillageVoice.com. November 9, 2011.

Swickey, Zachary. "A Drake Performance for $250k? That's a Steal," MTV News. May 8, 2011.

Taylor, Sarah. "Drake Talks Young Love with Keshia Chanté," MuchMusic.com. May 20, 2009.

The-weeknd.com.

TMZ Staff. "Drake — I'm One of the Best Jews of All Time," TMZ.com. February 9, 2011.

———. "Drake Targeted in Massive Concert Scam," TMZ.com. April 6, 2011.

———. "Matisyahu — Drake Can't Compare to my Jewness," TMZ. com. February 16, 2011.

TorontoRappers.com. Big Page interview. http://www .torontorappers.com/component/content/article/1-latest-news/1-big-page-interview.html.

Trapunski, Richard. "Q & A: Melanie Fiona Talks Her Teen Years with Drake, Moving to the U.S. to Find Success, and Playing the Genre Game," Aux.tv. April 11, 2012.

T-RexXx. *Rap City*. January 13, 2011. http://blog.muchmusic.com/
    watch-rapcitys-full-interview-with-drake/.

"T. Slack: The Big Picture," CorporateTakeover. December 24, 2007.
    http://corporatetakeover.wordpress.com/2007/12/24/ct-
    exclusive-interview-with-the-ceo-of-bigger-picture-
    entertainment/.

Tucker, Ken. "Grammy U: Conversation with Drake," Ocean Way
    Studio, Nashville, Tennessee. November 19, 2009.

Twitter.com/bamnproductions.

Twitter.com/Drake.

Twitter.com/Ovo40.

Twitter.com/Trexxx1loveto.

Twitter.com/TheWeekndxo.

Urb Staff. "Drake: the Complete Interview — Unedited
    Transcript," Urb.com. June 15, 2009.

Vanderbilt University Staff. "Q & A with Drake," InsideVandy.com.
    November 28, 2009.

VladTV.com

Weiner, Jonah. "Weed, Top Chefs and Rick Ross: Drake Ranges
    Wide on New Album," *Rolling Stone*. August 4, 2011.

Welch, Will. "Breakout: Drake," *GQ*. December 2010.

Wheeler, Brad. "Drake and Big Page: The beef, the diss and the
    Tweet," *Globe and Mail*. June 18, 2010.

Williams, Wes & Hendricks-Williams, Tamara. *Stick To Your Vision*.
    Toronto: McClelland & Steward, 2010.

WorldStarHipHop.com.

"Young Money CEO Cortez Bryant Talks Wayne Vs. Drake +
    Drizzy's 5th Single," Vibe.com. August 30, 2010.

YouTube.com/drakevevo.

Ziegbe, Mawuse. "Nicki Minaj and Drake End Twitter Marriage,"
    MTV.com. August 29, 2010.

Acknowledgments

A special thanks to the ECW Press crew for presenting me with this opportunity. London Jen Hale for making it happen and "getting it." JD for being JD. Jen Knoch and Crissy Boylan for editorially reining in the free-spiritedness that is Dalton. Troy Cunningham and Rachel Ironstone for their design and production work. Alexis Van Straten for pushing the Daltoganda. And the Ontario Arts Council's Writers Reserve program for supporting this work.

Bless up to Ill Will Strickland for putting me on to Drake. And to the Toronto hip hop pioneers (not lie-oneers) who paved the way and created the conditions for there to be a Drake. We all stand on the shoulders of those who came before us. This list is not conclusive (that would require another book length ode) but is comprised of people I know, worked and/or "reasoned" with, learned from, travelled and hung out with, who mentored me, whose art inspired me and the rest. If I left your name out, it's only because these deadlines have left my brain scattered and I'd need another 11–15 pages to truly thank every one of you who has made a difference.

Junior (Monica's), Ebony Sound Crew's Eddie Williams & Willie D, Sunshine Sound Crew's Tony D, JC, Brother Different a.k.a. Vanilla Nice / the original Eminem, K4CE and moms Morrison, HDV a.k.a. Jacky Jasper a.k.a. P.I.M.P of the worldwideweb, Butch Lee, Desmond and Orville (Jungle mentors), Maceo Sound Crew, City Crew, DJ Carl Allen, 2 Rude, Rumble and Strong, Ghetto Concept (all day, every day), Thrust, DJ X (Adrien), Johnbronski, Ivan Berry, Thrust, Nu Black Nation's Thando, Motion, DJ Power and fam, Nasty Howie T, Maestro Wes, UBAD, Ice, Big C, Sweet Ebony, Big Al and Altraxx, Chris Jackson a.k.a. DJ Jel, "Mr. Metro" Devon (and Jay Martin), Michie Mee and crew, Farley Flex, Julian Arthur and Groove-a-lot Records, Ron Nelson, The Terrace (bounce, skate!), Roller World, Skate Palace, Party Centre, Concert Hall and the legendary "25 Cent" dances (that many snuck into and/or took back door entry despite the cost!).

And big ups to the millennial hip hop generationers doing it now and leading us Black to the Future: there's my fellow Oakwood alumni everywhere, from way back when (Motion, DJ X, DJ Power) to now (Ian "Kamau," SPIN El Poeta, Boonaa Mohammed, T-RexXx, Chantle Beeso). Kehinde Bah and Taiwo Twin, Che Kothari, Marwan Lucas, Chevy x King & The Real Voyce, Fred E Fame, Jason

Richards Young Dun, DJ Nana and Roomie Rich Kidd, DJ L'oqenz, Amanda "32 C" Parris . . . the list goes on and on.

And a shout out to *some* of my peoples doing good work. Aisha Wickham, Agile, Al St. Louis, Dr. Althea Prince, Alton Morgan, Dwight Drummond, Emily & Lekan (and the hot new babe), Jay Pitter, Stacey Mckenzie, NICE (Andrew Francis, Jonathan 1 Bunce and Jonathan 2 Shedletzky), Ashante Infantry, David Clickety Click & Saidah Baba Talibah, Fennella Bruce, Freedome Bradley, Adrian Eccleston, Kevin "Jedi" Barton, Ricky Black, Natty B/Empress and Jah Chosen, Kheaven Only Knows, Palma and G (Bulletproof), Golden Child, Massa T and Paula, Gee Wunder(works), IRS, Brass Munk, Mindbender Tha Mayor, Jay Devonish, Neil Armstrong, Barry Hibbert, Reuben Coward, Tara Chase, Roshaniuk Jaberi, Bsose, Leroy "Ras" King, Lava Man, Peculiar I, Paul Martin, 4th Pyramid, Rasheeda Riley, Red 1 Romeo, Remi Warner and Warner familia, Ed Ratiarason and family, Tasha Rosez, Andy Williams, Afrakaren and Tuku, Saada Branker, Ryan Bailey, TAJ Tha Black Lion, Nick Davis, Telmary Diaz, Franz Thomas, P-Frank Williams, Griz on the Grind, Ernie Paniccioli, Wolde / Chelvin and Ethiopian Orthodox, Brother Jerone and N.O.I, Dawn Langfield, Daymon Green(berg), Ivan Evidente / Jody Laraya and the Five Swift Household, Jay Douglas, Nylda Lady Noyz, Owen Gordon, Eric Alper, Dr. Ken Montague, Kwame, The Real Solange, John Kong, JuLION / Canadian Reggae World, Big Poppa Jelani "J-Wyze" and fam, Wallo Judah, Kardinal (H) offishall and my man Maydizzle, Lava Man, The Baileys (Cameron / Maxine), Velma Morgan, Karen Carter, and Marvel (where Covert Opps @?).

To my Marlee Avenue and Little Jamaica foundation. Mark Smith and Smith Clan, Wayne / Ruthven and the Blake Clan, Charles/Bernard and the Lewis Clan, Dane "Doobie" / Gary and fam, every barbershop along Eglinton Ave. where I know most everyone on a first name basis and to my More Than a Haircut Crew who hold down Eglinton Avenue on the first weekend of every month (Shaka Zulu, Big Daddy Robbie, Peculiar I, Lorraine and Jomo Rainbow Ross, Theresa, Susan, Sherri, Sharon).

I didn't come to bow either (I came to conquer)
— Daltpak Chopra a.k.a. Usain Dalt

I am the internet and I am the winternet.
And they don't see nothing yet!
— Lee Scratch Perry